WITHDRAWN

An Iowa Schoolma'am

A
BUR
OAK
BOOK

An Iowa Schoolma'am

LETTERS OF

Elizabeth "Bess" Corey, 1904–1908

EDITED BY

PHILIP L. GERBER

AND

CHARLOTTE M. WRIGHT

FOREWORD BY

PAUL THEOBALD

University of Iowa Press

Iowa City

University of Iowa Press,
Iowa City 52242
Copyright © 2011 by the
University of Iowa Press
www.uiowapress.org
Printed in the United States
of America

Design by Richard Hendel

No part of this book may be
reproduced or used in any
form or by any means without
permission in writing from
the publisher. All reasonable
steps have been taken to
contact copyright holders of
material used in this book. The
publisher would be pleased to
make suitable arrangements
with any whom it has not
been possible to reach.
Unattributed photographs
are from the collection of
Philip L. Gerber, now located
in Special Collections at the
State Historical Society, Iowa
City, Iowa.

The University of Iowa Press is a
member of Green Press Initiative and
is committed to preserving natural
resources.

Printed on acid-free paper

Library of Congress
Cataloging-in-Publication Data
Corey, Elizabeth.
An Iowa schoolma'am: letters of Elizabeth "Bess"
Corey, 1904–1908 / edited by Philip L. Gerber and
Charlotte M. Wright; foreword by Paul Theobald.
p.   cm.
Includes bibliographical references and index.
ISBN-13: 978-1-58729-960-5 (pbk.)
ISBN-10: 1-58729-960-7 (pbk.)
ISBN-13: 978-1-58729-961-2 (e-book)
ISBN-10: 1-58729-961-5 (e-book)
1. Corey, Elizabeth—Correspondence.
2. Teachers—Iowa—Correspondence. 3. Rural
schools—Iowa. I. Gerber, Philip L. II. Wright,
Charlotte M. III. Title.
LA2317.C63417A4 2011
371.10092—dc22
[B]   2010043601

To PHIL GERBER, *whose untiring dedication to Bachelor Bess ensured that these letters would see the light of day, and to* PAUL COREY, *who gave Phil these letters in 1989*

Contents

Foreword PAUL THEOBALD

This collection of letters written by farm-girl turned schoolma'am Elizabeth "Bess" Corey extends from October 1904 to August 1908. The letters, written mostly to her mother and siblings back on the farm in Marne, Iowa, collectively tell a story about rural life and living in Iowa at the very start of the twentieth century. More specifically, they reveal the possibilities and limitations faced by young rural women at that time. Looming large among those very few possibilities was a career as a country school teacher. Although it would not have been her first choice, that career became central to the life of Elizabeth Corey. She would try her hand at many other things over the years, but she always went back to teaching. The letters in this book precede those that were collected and published in a similar and earlier volume, *Bachelor Bess: The Homesteading Letters of Elizabeth Corey, 1909–1919*, edited by Philip L. Gerber, letters that focused on Elizabeth Corey's unusual decision to strike out on her own, at age twenty-one, to homestead in central South Dakota.

An Iowa Schoolma'am tells a story that is more conventional than the first one and is far more typical of young rural women in the Midwest. There were few professions open to them as the twentieth century began and rural women, especially those born and raised on farms, had even fewer options than did their urban counterparts. Acquiring a high school education was a difficult proposition for farm youth, who could not easily travel to and from a high school each day. And, in any event, mass attendance at American high schools was still years away. In 1904, across the country, perhaps two in ten high school–age youth actually attended one. Among farm children, the percentage was undoubtedly smaller. By 1913, just a few years after the last letter in this collection was sent, one of every two American students attended one of the nation's 212,000 single-teacher schools.[1] The total in Iowa, however, was much greater. In fact, as late as 1936, 77 percent of Iowa's school children were attending one of the nearly 9,000 one-room schools.[2]

In the fall of 1904, Bess moved from her home farm near Marne to Walnut, Iowa, to begin the ninth grade and perhaps to move all the

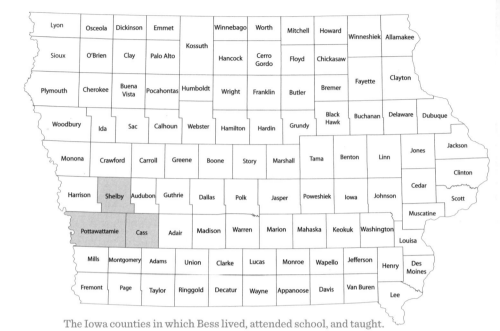

The Iowa counties in which Bess lived, attended school, and taught.

way through a high school program. Walnut was seven miles from Corey Farm—a considerable distance in a world without automobiles. Her only option was to pay a Walnut family, in this case the Copleys, for providing her room and board. This common practice was a source of added income for the residents of towns large enough to support a high school. Indeed, it was not uncommon for farm children attending high school to board with town families as late as the 1940s and even into the 1950s. While automobiles were plentiful by this time, they were not dependable in snow, and local governments did not ordinarily have the necessary equipment to keep rural roads open during winter. When conditions became especially bad, neighbors often got together to dig out the worst areas—those susceptible to high drifts—by hand. Bess makes reference to such an occasion while living in Walnut and attending ninth grade.

In point of fact, it is the everyday references throughout Elizabeth Corey's letters that make this collection such a clear window to rural history generally, and rural education history in particular. There is not a single rural school dynamic—be it corporal punishment, parental involvement, recitation pedagogy, student behavior, or curriculum—that does not surface in these letters, making this book an invaluable historical resource on many levels. For instance, it is possible to see Bess steadily develop greater wherewithal as a grammarian and a speller as the years go by, although she began her teaching career in 1905 with literacy skills that would not be acceptable today.

As the common school system evolved in the nineteenth century, a teacher certification system was developed that could be administered by the county's superintendent of instruction. Although there were slight differences from state to state, and sometimes even within each state, there were generally three gradations of teaching certificates: first, second, and third grade, although the names had nothing to do with the way the term "grade" has since been applied to a student's progress through school. Throughout the years captured by these wonderful letters, Bess was never able to acquire anything other than the very lowest teaching certificate, that of third grade. At the very end of the collection is a letter in which she admits to her mother that after taking the exam yet again, she "only got a third—too low in Grammar and physiology."

In truth, Bess was not what we would today consider well educated. Months after starting the ninth grade in Walnut, she was forced to quit and return home due to the unexpected death of her father in February, 1905. That summer, however, she moved to Harlan, Iowa, boarded with the Stewart family, took summer school classes, and attended a "teacher's institute" there. Teacher's institutes were short-term pedagogical workshops that served as a kind of continuing education for certified teachers and a kind of teacher preparation for those, like Bess in the summer of 1905, who wished to become certified. It was the task of the county superintendent to schedule and orchestrate these institutes in various forms throughout the county so that teachers would not be prohibited from attending due to distance from their homes. The two- or three-week institute was often an exciting time in the small towns of Iowa and other states. Town residents busily readied their homes to take on boarders (a welcome income source for the residents), and to enjoy live music, countless picnics and gatherings that multiplied while the teachers, and prospective teachers, were in town.

In Johnson County, Iowa, in the early twentieth century, a county school superintendent kept meticulous records of the early twentieth-century teacher's institutes he orchestrated, giving scholars and education historians some insights into the system. He recorded that the average attendance was 70, ninety percent of whom were female. The average age of all attendees was 19.7 years, while the average length of teaching service prior to attending the institute was 2.7 terms—or a little over one year of teaching. Twenty-eight percent had been to a Johnson County teacher's institute offered the year before, leaving 72 percent as first-time attendees.[3] While teacher's institutes were still fairly well attended during the first couple of decades of the twentieth century, they were gradually being replaced by a system of pre-service and in-service teacher education. Many rural high schools created "normal departments," where young people (typically women) could prepare for a teaching career in area country schools. But increasingly the school boards, encouraged by ever more insistent state departments of education, sought to hire teachers who had finished post–high school normal training, most often a one-year program at a regional normal college.

As was the case for Bess in several successive summers, local high schools concluded their summer school offerings so that students could avail themselves of the teacher's institute that generally followed the summer session. In this manner, Bess made only slow progress toward a high school diploma. Despite her educational deficiencies, she became a competent teacher. In fact, it wasn't until 1927, nearly twenty years after the last of the letters in this collection, and after a lifelong teaching career, that she finally earned her high school diploma.

Bess was seventeen years old when she attended summer school and the teacher's institute in Harlan the summer after her father died. Despite her youth, she desperately wanted to pass the exam so that she could teach in the fall and contribute to the meager income her widowed mother received from working a 160-acre farm alongside her seven children. Because some superintendents objected to anyone under eighteen taking the teacher certification exam, Bess wrote to her mother asking if she might tell "a little white lie" by listing her age as eighteen. Later, however, she wrote, "I didn't have the grit to give my age [as] 18." Her letters reveal a common suspicion that not all county superintendents were on the up and up when it came to extending certification. Other test-takers advised Bess to change her name to "O'Corey," as "you'll get a certificate if you're Irish, even if you don't know beans." Another shared that "a $10 bill will fetch a certificate quicker than brains."

Bess changed neither her name nor her age and still managed to get a "temporary" certificate that would serve until she turned eighteen. Her first teaching position was near Tennant, Iowa, about five miles west of Harlan and about twenty miles from Corey Farm. Bess boarded with a farm family by the name of Weaver (or, as she spells it, "Wever") for most of this teaching stint. More than likely, the school district paid the Weavers for boarding Bess. Beyond that, Bess is likely to have received somewhere between $35 and $50 per month while the school term lasted. Bess seldom mentions her salary, though there are many references to sending large chunks of it back to her mother. Sometimes school districts spread the burden of "boarding the teacher," creating a schedule that could consist of as little as one week in each household. Because this was very unpopular among teachers, school districts gradually discovered that the practice of "boarding around" limited the number of candidates for teaching positions at their school.

Sometimes several families wanted the extra income that came from boarding the teacher, but sometimes, too, it was tough to find a family willing to do it at all. Bess wrote home about an acquaintance who was looking as far as two and three miles from the school to find a family willing to take her. Personality clashes, "parenting" philosophies, even religious allegiances sometimes made boarding the teacher a trying experience for all involved. A young Lutheran girl teaching in a North Dakota one-room school confided in her diary that she worried about boarding with a Catholic family. When her first Sunday arrived and she was asked by her hosts if she wanted to attend mass, she replied, "I was told that if a Lutheran came into a Catholic church, when the Lutheran went out, they'd wash the pews." "Oh my no," replied her host, and this boarding arrangement proved to be satisfactory to all.[4]

Sometimes host families made what seemed to the teacher to be excessive demands, like the Copleys with whom Bess once boarded. This family expected her to help with chores on the weekend. Bess frequently helped with the milking, but not all teachers were willing to put up with what they deemed to be unwarranted work demands. Even when Bess boarded with a family member, her Aunt Jennie, she had "run-ins" with her uncle, who accused her of eating too much and using too much heating oil to keep her room warm. Difficulties like these were common, but there were few alternatives to this traditional arrangement. Changes were on the horizon, however, and Bess's letters reveal ample evidence of this. The telephone, electric lights, rural free mail delivery, and indoor plumbing were all slowly making their way into rural life in Iowa during the first decade of the new century. Even the practice of boarding was showing signs of transition. At one point Bess writes to her mother that she and a friend were considering "hiring a room" and "boarding" themselves, meaning they would rent a room to sleep in and provide food for themselves—which would have been a significant change in the usual living arrangements for single women at that time.

By 1905, when Bess began her country school teaching career, female teachers were more numerous by far than their male counterparts. The profession was feminizing quickly, compared to nineteenth-century circumstances. Horace Mann of Massachusetts, the nation's first state superintendent of instruction, had argued at the inception of the free school system in 1836 that women ought to be courted for the nation's teaching force. Mann had been to Prussia, where the teaching population was predominantly female, and he was impressed with the way they nurtured young children rather than utilizing the typically cold, distant, and strict pedagogy common at the time. He therefore believed women were better suited for teaching because they were nurturers by nature. On top of this, according to Mann, they had the added benefit of being cheaper to employ than males.

From a twenty-first-century vantage point, gender-differentiated pay for the same work seems out of step. But at the beginning of the twentieth century, it was rarely questioned. The general cultural assumption was that males were or would become heads of households, while women would always play a subordinate economic role. It stood to reason, then, that pay rates ought to differ, and they did. In Clark County, Illinois, one individual served as a school board clerk for seventeen years, from 1862 to 1879. During that time he kept a careful record of the teachers who taught each school term, and how much they were paid. Nineteenth-century rural schools generally held two terms, summer and winter, because farm work slowed to some degree during these times. For the seventeen years during which this Clark County gentleman served as clerk, two teaching contracts were signed each year, for a total of thirty-four. Of this number, twenty were signed by males, and fourteen by females. Over this seventeen-year period, female teachers averaged $17 per month in wages, while their male counterparts averaged $33 per month.[5]

Throughout the Midwest there was a marked preference for males to teach the winter terms. Winter was the time of year with the least amount of farm work, and consequently the older male students, the "big boys" as Bess would refer to them, were more often in attendance. These older boys often skipped summer terms entirely, making a more hospitable teaching environment for a young female teacher, at least according to the popular cultural assumptions of the era. One of the pranks school board members thought they might avoid by hiring male teachers, a prank generally attributed to big boys, was "turning the teacher out." This happened when students physically picked up the teacher, ignored her protests, and carried her outside of the school, whereupon the students would rush back in and lock the door. This phenomenon was common enough to be mentioned in one of Bess's letters home. She describes how one of the older men in the community used candy to bribe the students in an effort to get them to turn Bess out of her school. Luckily for Bess, the bribery didn't work.

As the nineteenth century ended, increasing pressure was put on rural schools to begin to mimic the kind of nine-month school calendar that was fast becoming the norm in town and city schools. A careful reading of Bess's letters reveals that while rural Iowa schools held on to the two-term concept, the dates of these terms began shifting toward the fall and spring. By 1931, Iowa, like most states, had adopted the nine-month calendar for all schools. Data concerning salaries at this time reveal America's cultural infatuation with what nearly everyone came to believe would be an urban future. If you were a teacher in a rural one-room school in 1931, your average salary would have been approximately $874 per school year, less than half of what city teachers earned.[6] Many regional normal-schools-turned-teacher-colleges, like La Crosse State in Wisconsin, maintained two teacher-preparation tracks by the 1920s and 30s. If you wanted to teach in city schools, you followed a two-year course of study. If you were content to teach in country schools, a one-year course of study was deemed to be sufficient—a circumstance that clearly betrays a far-reaching cultural embrace of urban superiority.

It was this cultural ethos that fueled the long and incessant drive for country school consolidation that began almost at the outset of the twentieth century and continued all the way to its end. In what is sometimes called the first school consolidation west of the Mississippi River, residents around Buffalo Township in Winnebago County, Iowa, voted to collapse several country schools into a single independent district in the village of Buffalo Center in 1895.[7] Several similar consolidations followed during the first decade of the twentieth century, but in general Iowa and other midwestern states remained slow to close country schools, despite increasing political pressure to do so. For example, as early as 1925, nineteen states had passed laws to encourage country schools to consolidate.[8] In the wake of a pronounced rural to urban demographic shift and the concomitant city majority in state legislatures, the political pressure picked up considerably. By 1980, Iowa's one-room schools were all but gone.

As one-room schools at the start of the twentieth century began the gradual shift to the city school calendar, the growing domination of women in the country school teaching ranks became even more pronounced. Males were deemed to be more productive than females, from an economic standpoint, on the typical farmstead. Both fall and spring contained labor-intensive months, with soil preparation and planting in the spring, and harvest in the fall. Because male teachers were often needed at home, they tended to teach only when they could acquire a contract for a school close to where they lived and farmed. While it was not totally unheard of, male teachers were also less likely to board with another family.

Because the number of one-room school districts was still growing during the first decade of the twentieth century, because the traditional nineteenth-century school-term calendar was gradually shifting, and because males were reluctant to teach in schools that would take them too far from where their farm labor was needed and they were reluctant to board with another family when they did teach, females began to outnumber males as country school teachers by a considerable margin. By 1900, nearly 75 percent of all teachers in the United States were women. If the count had been limited to one-room schools, the percentage would have been higher. In 1916, as an example, 85 percent of all teachers in North Dakota one-room schools were women.[9]

Elizabeth Corey's letters clearly demonstrate that "teacher turnover" was the norm, not the exception. In the years covered by these letters, Bess never taught in the same school for two successive terms. It should be noted, too, that the teaching profession during the nineteenth and early twentieth centuries was limited to males and *single* females. As soon as young women married they were considered ineligible for teaching positions, as was the case with Bess's own mother. This would begin to change slowly during the 1910s, especially in sparse areas, like the Dakotas, where it was difficult to secure the services of a teacher at all.

Bess's letters also reveal what happens in a society that limits the possibilities for various segments of the population. Bess became a teacher because it was virtually the only avenue through which she, as a female, might generate income in an effort to help her widowed mother make ends meet. On more than one occasion she reminds her mother that teaching would not have been her first choice of professions. She wrote that she would "rather stay at home and raise chickens, make garden, and slop hogs than teach school." Indeed, as soon as she turned twenty-one, Bess traveled to central South Dakota to file a homestead claim. Try as she might, however, it never proved profitable, so Bess remained close to the teaching profession for her entire working life.

This is not to suggest that Bess was anything other than a dedicated, capable teacher, which she clearly was. The general reader interested in the life of one-room schools will encounter a wonderful first-hand description of just that from these letters. In them is an account of creative pedagogy that included gardening with her students, after-hour or weekend picnics and socials, and various other events that demonstrate the centrality of one-room schools to neighborhood life. And, of course, negative aspects of the country school experience are here as well. Bess reports "trouble with parents" now and then and even in one instance kept a score of sorts, reporting the number of local families that were for her, and the number against. Later she wrote that she guessed "there is about the same number of kickers in each neighborhood."

The historian of education will also find subtle references to issues of considerable interest. For example, in her formal role as teacher, Bess clearly passed along prevalent racial stereotypes concerning blacks, and although her motive does not seem malevolent, her words are startling to read in the context of today's standards. In one instance she records that she put two of her students in black-face to play "little niggers" in a school program. In another instance, she wrote to her mother about the suspiciously cordial behavior of the children of a parent with whom she had had difficulties, relaying that she suspected "a nigger in the fence." Ethnic stereotypes also crept into these letters. For example, Bess frequently pokes fun at the speech and behavior of Danish families living in the districts where she taught.

On one occasion Bess traveled to see the county superintendent to ask what might be done about parents who refused to provide the appropriate schoolbooks for their children. Unlike other states, Iowa still had not passed a free textbook law (something that would come in the next decade), meaning that children would sometimes study from books that were very old or they might have no books at all. As one might expect, this was an enormous hardship for teachers, but Bess, like other teachers, received no particularly helpful advice from the superintendent.

This collection of letters is a wonderful inside look at a bygone era. To cite just a few more of many possible examples, these letters clearly reveal that doctors were a last resort when it came to health care; that clothes were most often homemade—lovingly, and with care and skill; that the county poor farm was a possible destination for those who could not support themselves; that courting was a ritualized affair (often including "walking alone with a man" or "driving in the country"); and that family and community held strong and enduring values in rural society. We are fortunate that Bess's mother, Margaret Corey, saved these wonderful letters; that Paul Corey, Bess's youngest sibling (who, by the way, became an accomplished novelist and writer), consented to make them available for a twenty-first-century audience; and that Phil Gerber labored for years to bring all of Bess's marvelous letters to light.

NOTES

1. Jonathan Zimmerman, *Small Wonder: The Little Red Schoolhouse in History and Memory* (New Haven: Yale University Press, 2009), 17.

2. William L. Sherman, ed., *Iowa's Country Schools: Landmarks of Learning* (Des Moines: Iowa State Education Association and Mid-Prairie Books, 1998), 9.

3. Paul Theobald, *Call School: Rural Education in the Midwest to 1918* (Carbondale: Southern Illinois University Press, 1995), 149.

4. Theobald, 122.

5. Theobald, 94.

6. Zimmerman, 101.

7. Sherman, 5.

8. Zimmerman, 47.

9. Zimmerman, 29.

RECOMMENDED READING

Fraser, James W. *Preparing America's Teachers: A History*. New York: Teachers College Press, 2006.

Fuller, Wayne E. *The Old Country School: The Story of Rural Education in the Middle West*. Chicago: University of Chicago Press, 1982.

Ogren, Christine A. *The American State Normal School: An Instrument of Great Good*. New York: Palgrave Macmillan, 2005.

Reynolds, David R. *There Goes the Neighborhood: Rural School Consolidation at the Grass Roots in Early Twentieth-Century Iowa*. Iowa City: University of Iowa Press, 1999.

Sherman, William L., ed. *Iowa's Country Schools: Landmarks of Learning*. Des Moines: Iowa State Education Association and Mid-Prairie Books, 1998.

Theobald, Paul. *Call School: Rural Education in the Midwest to 1918*. Carbondale: Southern Illinois University Press, 1995.

Zimmerman, Jonathan. *Small Wonder: The Little Red Schoolhouse in History and Memory*. New Haven: Yale University Press, 2009.

Preface PHILIP L. GERBER

The eighty-four letters in this collection likely include every note that
Elizabeth "Bess" Corey wrote to her family back at Corey Farm, in
Marne, Cass County, Iowa, between 1904 and 1908, while she was
away from home either attending classes or teaching school. Like
the letters she would write to her mother and siblings from South
Dakota once she became a homesteader—chronicled in *Bachelor
Bess: The Homesteading Letters of Elizabeth Corey, 1909-1919*, which
I published in 1990—these letters entertain while they inform, as
they were intended to do, and they were prized by her family. Bess's
youngest brother, Paul Corey, remembered their being read aloud to
the assembled family at supper so that their continuing saga, written
decades before the arrival of radio and television, became the family's
own "private soap opera."

The great majority of these letters are addressed "Dear Mamma"
and signed "Your little girl Bess," but their contents were intended
for sharing with all. Bess's mother, Margaret Corey, who had herself
been a schoolmarm in Cass County, Iowa, in the 1880s, preserved her
daughter's correspondence methodically, each one laid away safely
in its own delivery envelope (the backs of which often provided space
for Mrs. Corey's impromptu shopping lists or the preliminary notes
and trivia on which her replies would be based—things to be sure
to tell Bess). The few letters addressed to Bess's older brother Olney
eventually became part of Mrs. Corey's accumulation as well, and a
number of Bess's enclosures—bits of sample fabric, ribbons worn on
special occasions, sketches by Bess or by some of her pupils, or their
photographs—were retained in the envelopes along with the letters
themselves.

Evidence in these letters assures us that Bess was an inveterate
writer, habitually involved with half a dozen or more correspondents
at any given moment, several of whom she might write to at a single
sitting. Even at two cents a stamp, her postage expenditures seemed
prodigious enough to warrant her commenting on them from time
to time. She mentions writing not only to her relatives (Grandma
Corey, Aunt Jennie, Uncle John) but to childhood friends such as
Mary Lanigan and Valerie Harris—or women such as Ida Wever, a

friend she met in Tennant who then moved to Missouri—and Anna and Sarah Stewart of the huge extended Stewart clan of Harlan, but none of these letters survived.

Besides providing a many-stranded portrait of their writer, Bess Corey's youthful letters reveal the evolution of a genuinely skilled writer. We observe Bess as she begins writing while still in school, an innocent and wholly untrained neophyte writer; we watch as she develops a marked degree of sophistication. She takes her first, tentative steps at sixteen, stumbling rather frequently. But being an astute observer, she learns as she goes forward, so that when she leaves Iowa at age twenty-one Bess has traveled a good distance toward becoming a journeyman letter-writer well prepared to practice her craft.

Bess closes her very first letter with the comment: "Could write enough to fill a book if I had time." In an intuitive way she seems to understand already that she possesses much in the way of materials for writing, but that as yet she knows virtually nothing of how she must use these materials to advantage; she has no technique. It is apparent that her daily activities will furnish the substance for her pen. Later, a practicing teacher in the field, Bess remarks that she would stuff all the strange, surprising things that were happening to her into a journal—if only she had a book to do it in. But she never would possess such a book, and she must not have really wanted one, for if she had she could easily have walked to the nearest stationer's (the same establishment that supplied her letter paper) and procured a proper blank book at minimal expense. For her, letters were journal enough—and sufficed for diary as well. Whatever she wanted to preserve or relay to others went down on the pages of her letters, for what Bess wanted most when far from home base was an opportunity to converse with her family members and her friends, and for that purpose the letter form was close to being ideal. She liked to complain of the continual expense of paper and postage, expenses that did tend to strain her chronic money problem, but she would gladly have gone without supper to afford them.

A fascinating aspect of Bess's letters concerns their revelation of her learning process in the use of the English tongue. Her first letters betray a near-total bewilderment at the use, for instance, of the apostrophe, not to mention the niceties to be achieved through comma, period, and semicolon. Her system of capitalization is in chaos. And grammar at times seems a foreign tongue. Of her spelling we will not speak (except to mention that with time it improves).

The first letters, composed of truncated sentences hastily jotted down, concern topics that are raised only to remain stranded stillborn on the page awaiting the life-giving breath of development that never arrives. "The boys had three visitors" and "I am baking bread today" are telegraphic, basic but anemic and unsatisfying. They do little credit to the writer and do not nourish the reader. It was not long, however, before Bess began to learn the knack of providing those telling details that could revive a faltering notation and cause it to spring to life. How much more satisfying is: "John Eggerstodt and Ernest Feldhahn look so much like the pictures of Sunny Jim that the girls call him that, and Ernest is tall, good looking, serious and stylish from his barbercut hair to his patent leather shoes." Here Bess takes indispensable steps toward providing word snapshots that create images for her reader. She is in control of her medium. She is, at last, *writing*.

Whether Bess's improvement stemmed from questions fired at her from Corey Farm or was prompted by friendly but pointed suggestions offered by teachers at Walnut School, Bess came somehow to understand that she could better share her new life in Walnut by relating brief anecdotes that stemmed from the essence of her daily round; many of them are actually plotted stories—minuscule, of the briefest nature—but stories nevertheless. These tales sometimes employ Bess herself as observing narrator, standing on the fringe of the action, but in the more memorable accounts she occupies the center, becoming herself the heroine of a story whose events and subsidiary characters revolve around the focus that her activities create.

The tools of her trade were conundrums to Bess when she first began to put pen to paper. Her grammar-school education at #9 Clay Township School must have been rudimentary at best, and that would be no surprise, really, since the farmers' children were taught by whatever young lady with a state certificate in hand might happen to stroll down the pike (and if no one happened along, then for a term there would be no instruction at all—it was that simple). Bess in the beginning scarcely knew how to properly begin and end a sentence, let alone being possessed of any ability to control her creation as it skipped along the page under its own power. Her impulse always was for the oral, not the written, yet that impulse for the spoken word, in her case, proves to be an immense virtue, one that enlivens her eclectic style.

Bess's failure at first to command many of the basics of written discourse has its pleasant ironies, one of which is to lend her writing an authentic air of the *naif* that bears resemblance to some of the deliberately illiterate humorists of her day and the age immediately preceding—Josh Billings and his ilk come to mind (Walt Mason being one of Bess's favorites). The letters presented in this book retain Bess's sometimes unworldly spelling as well as other off-center practices. For the most part, her grammatical flaws present few obstacles for the reader. Examples of the phonetic spellings are: *conntrdict, fue* (few), *dosen't, wether* (weather or whether), *comming, alright, diging, suddent, skeered, stoped, steped, incloes (enclose), benifit, elboes, jurk,* and on and on. Bess struggles to name the chest of drawers in her rented room but it comes out *bereau* anyway—"close but no cigar," as she herself might comment in the flip lingo of her time. These are illiteracies, to be sure, but for an editor to step in with the intention somehow of "saving" Bess Corey from herself would be to destroy a precious aspect of her starting out. So it will remain quite clear to all readers that Bess spelled by ear, that at age sixteen she seems never to have heard of rules such as those for doubling consonants or for adding adverbial suffixes such as *ly*. Proceeding almost purely by sound (and therefore left prostrate at the mercy of local pronunciation), Bess invariably is guilty of misspelling the names of pupils and neighbors alike. In the classrooms of her early teaching years, surely, it was often the blind leading the blind.

Bess's writing is clearly a simple extension of the way she spoke. She is at her best when she has an exciting episode to relate; but like a hopped-up child who runs in from outdoors so full of her subject that everything tumbles out in one single incoherent gush, the whole tale expended in a single breath, Bess has to battle against her tendency to tell *all* in one recklessly racing sentence.

Fortunately, Bess was both alert and a quick study. A name she might misspell as she moves into a new school district is soon learned and thereafter appears in her letters in its proper form. A key role in any writer's improvement is played by the admission that one's work is flawed, and by the desire to make improvement. Bess many times in her letters admits to her flaws, sometimes throwing up her hands in despair as to how a word or name is to be managed. But knowledge becomes power, and gradually (never entirely) the misspellings disappear from her pages, her sentences are reined in, her punctuation regularized. It seems likely that a knowledgeable English teacher may have planted the right seeds for Bess upon her entry into Walnut School, or perhaps that her schoolteaching colleagues and correspondents, or the instructors at the Institutes she regularly attended, may have gently called her attention to her problems sufficiently to make her establish in her mind a permanent alert to the principle of self-correction.

A major sign of the oral style that animates Bess Corey's correspondence is her impulse to employ the colloquial tongue. Intuitively she went for the close-at-hand metaphors, utilizing the straightforward and colorful lingo of the farm and the hamlet that came like second nature to her. Bess was, after all, most definitely "of the people," moving, living, working all of her days among the most ordinary of country folk. As readers we soon become acclimatized to her employment of informalities, even of slang expressions, which are much more easily tolerated by readers today than they were in her own, more formal time. It has worked in her favor that the national linguistic trend has swung toward simplicity and informality. Because discrete terms in the American language have a persistent way of sneaking their way up the ladder of respectability, we might forget that a word like *swell* was disapproved of socially in 1904 (which is when Bess uses it), to say nothing of her truly aberrant version *swellest*. But, approve of or frown at her diction, we must recognize the authenticity of her impulse.

At times Bess demonstrates a fine touch of writerly self-awareness, which she shows by enclosing her informalities in quotation marks, as in "There was 'somethin big' down there," but we are more likely to encounter informal terms that remain unidentified as such, slangy locutions like these: *guying* (joking), *lunker* (something heavy, stupid), to *rubber* (to turn and stare at something; to gawk), *duds* (clothing), *roasted* (criticized strongly), *go to roost* (go to bed for the night). Constructions such as these add color to Bess's writing, as do other slang phrases and homely thrusts at metaphor. These examples are representative: he is some punkins; my Sunday go to Preachin clothes; you can bet your Sunday shirt; it knocked the socks off me; I rec'd a joehummy of a postal card; slick as a greased pig; that fetched my English [temper] up; spair chink [spare change]; a stemwinder of a test; he was swelled up like fifty cents in a new suit and hat.

As she evolved into a more sophisticated writer (without ever loosening the finger she held on the common pulse), Bess became practiced at making more calculated use of the informalities of oral language that she heard on every side. She learned to employ such language for its double meanings, locating links between literal and figurative meanings that were intended to entertain even a moderately attentive reader, as in her remark that the playground sandburs that her barefooted students stepped on at recess made her school a "howling success." The humorous spin on words carries the day when Bess-the-skeptic refers to revival-meeting converts as "convicts" or when she reports that upon a visit to a friend's house "the Smith's bee saluted me on the cheek." She has a keen sense of the clever and develops it. Her use of the pun becomes endemic. Instinct leads the way, as in her spin on a friend's remark that in Bess the school district surely is getting something *great*. Such transparent self-references to her increasing poundage more than once come in for ironic treatment, as in "I weigh 220 pounds now, aint that dandy?" Irony for her becomes an habitual tool, as when Bess refers to "my gracious apartment" (the reader knows it for the tiny, jam-packed space it is) or in her reference to "the great city of Tennant" (scarcely even a hamlet).

Bess's account of a visit to the dentist demonstrates her intuitive control of the hyperbolic:

He got his hatchets and things ground up and then went to work. He cut out a piece of my gum about the size of your foot, then after cutting the rest of my gum free from the tooth he put that what you call it of his in my mouth and took a hold of that tooth as if it was a bad boy. He wiggled and twisted it and pulled until he got tired of fooling and then he yanked it out. You aught to have heard the exclamation he made when it came out!

As Bess learned that for a writer, the meat of things lay in the details and that manner might well become more significant than matter, she took important early steps toward self-realization as an emergent artist in her chosen genre.

In addition to the ever-central and vital self-portrait of Bess that a reader takes from these letters comes a realization that whatever the place described, whoever the cast, whatever the event, the world one enters with Bess Corey is a very *real* world. It exists, and Bess is its avatar. This world she conjures up is most surely not the same world that the reader inhabits, nor is it even a world that the reader might wish to inhabit—but the people in it convince; they live and breathe with a powerful and seductive sense of actuality. The reader finds himself smiling, nodding *yes, yes, this is the way it must have been, precisely, this surely is what was said, this has to be the way things went, the very way these folks behaved back then, at that time, that place.* With a powerful persuasion, the words Bess commits to paper create belief, are credible, and engage the reader.

The reader who is interested in the social history of America or who is ready to be entertained by pieces of authentic Americana set down "live" by an observant young woman between 1904 and 1908 will be rewarded by much of value in Bess's letters. This voice from the past recaptures the shapes in vanished photographs: the daily round of life on a middling-sized Iowa family farm at the dawn of the twentieth century; the small-town phenomenon of the same place and time; the glory days of railroading; and other forgotten snatches of social custom and religious ferment from the midwestern generation that followed the pioneers.

Of notable value is the light that Bess is able to cast upon the teaching profession as it existed from 1904 to 1908, especially as schooling was practiced in midwestern rural areas hovering along the outer rim of "civilization" at the moment when the nation determined that, come what may, every American child (who someday would be expected to cast votes with a modicum of intelligence and understanding) was going to have access to a basic grammar-school education. And so the country-school tradition was born. What did these tiny, often isolated rural schools look like? Of what nature, what caliber were their students? How were their teachers trained and selected? What curricula were stressed? How much was a teacher paid? What were her living conditions? What was her position in society? All of these topics—and more—served as the common grist for Bess Corey's mill. In these letters such subjects are handled with an immediacy and a specificity that create their second permanent value, wherein one comes into possession of a veritable concordance of teaching in the one-room rural schoolhouse, a chapter of daily American life now closed and all but lost in the mists of history, to be found again only in letters such as these.

Editor's Note CHARLOTTE M. WRIGHT

After Phil Gerber's untimely death in 2005, Holly Carver, then director of the University of Iowa Press, asked if I would work toward
completing his project of publishing the Iowa letters of Elizabeth
"Bess" Corey, the woman Gerber had introduced us to in his book
*Bachelor Bess: The Homesteading Letters of Elizabeth Corey, 1909–
1919*. Eugenia Gerber, Phil's wife, generously agreed to this plan. I
had edited letter collections before, so I expected the task would be
relatively simple: check the typed copies of the letters against their
originals to verify the accuracy of the typescript, add a few more foot-
notes to identify people and events, edit Phil's introduction, create
an index, and *voilà*: instant prequel to *Bachelor Bess*. The wake-up
call came months later when several large boxes filled with the handwritten, typed originals and photocopies that Phil had gathered over
many years of research landed on my desk. Phil had immersed himself in the history of the southwestern Iowa communities where Bess
had grown up, attended school, and eventually taught in one-room
schoolhouses, and he had obviously hoped to write a detailed local
history that would place Bess's Iowa letters within the broader context of rural Iowa at the turn of the century.

My original plan was to retain Phil's expansive ideas for organizing
the book and placing the letters in a deep historical context, but as I
read through his notes and Bess's letters I began to realize that back-
tracking through his research would take several years — at which
point I would still not be the expert he was. In addition, I would have
to search for new documents and other primary sources that might
have come to light in the years since his death if I were to do justice
to the vision he had for the book. I decided to focus on what I found
most significant in the letters themselves: a first-person account of
the life of an Iowa schoolteacher at the turn of the twentieth century.
I asked education historian Paul Theobald to write a foreword sum-
marizing the state of the school system at that time and putting Bess's
letters into that context, then I edited Phil's original introduction to
retain his core contribution to understanding Bess Corey: the literary
analysis of the language Bess used in the letters.

Thus, the letters speak for themselves, revealing a young and vibrant and vulnerable Bess, first making her way through the training to become a teacher, and then interacting with her students and their parents and the other community members for each school in which she taught at the turn of the century. While *Bachelor Bess* and *An Iowa Schoolma'am* can be read as companion volumes, I also wanted to be sure this volume could stand alone as *Bachelor Bess* does, so I have included some of the background information on Bess and her family that is also found in the first book.

In formatting the letters for publication, these are the rules I followed. The dates, if not included on the letter itself, have been taken from the cancellation stamp on the envelope. Phil added headings to each letter to show whatever address is on the envelope, and I retained these headings unless the letter did not have an envelope, in which case I used just the date. Paragraph breaks are where Bess placed them, when that can be discerned from the letter itself. She didn't always indent, sometimes relying on the previous line ending somewhere short of the right margin to indicate that the next line should be a new paragraph. Words that Bess underlined have been set in italics. Bess used both "and" and "&," and I have left both as she wrote them. Phil's original transcripts modernized much of the punctuation and capitalization, but I reverted to Bess's original (and erratic) writing style, in part to show how she improved in language skills as she went through her schooling experiences. Bess's spelling has been retained in most cases; in only a few instances, where I thought it would help the reader, I added brackets around whatever material is not original to Bess. All endnotes were written by Phil Gerber unless the initials "CMW" are included in parentheses after them.

The preface that appears here is substantially shorter than the draft Phil Gerber left behind. I cut out large portions that duplicated what appears in *Bachelor Bess*, particularly information concerning Bess's early family life and her decision to move to South Dakota. Some details included in the preface have been moved either to endnotes—where they provide interesting annotations to names or events that Bess mentions—or to section headnotes, where they provide historical and cultural context to all the letters in that section. My intention was to retain Phil's own words and explanations wherever possible. Readers interested in Gerber's more substantive introduction, as well as the various articles he wrote and papers he presented about Elizabeth Corey, are directed to the State Historical Society of Iowa in Iowa City, where Eugenia Gerber has generously deposited the research results collected by her husband.

I am honored to have had the opportunity to edit this collection of letters. Strong, independent, and fearless, Bess Corey is just as much a role model for our time as she was in her day. All who have had the privilege of knowing and working with Phil Gerber miss his gentle wit, kind heart, and scholarly intensity.

Thanks are in order for many people who made this project possible. Eugenia Gerber has been patient while we made slow progress on her husband's project. Stacy Dreyer organized files, inventoried documents, proofread the original letters against the typescript copies, and did census research, among other duties. Cat Cassel also lent her proofreading skills. Mark Triana and John C. Kerpan made photocopies and kept the letters in order.

I am grateful to Special Collections at the State Historical Society of Iowa City, particularly Mary Bennett. As of the publication of this book, they now hold all the documents and photographs gathered by Philip Gerber in its preparation.

Corey Farm

During the early autumn of 1904 Edwin and Margaret (Brown) Corey went to south-central Missouri to investigate farmland, presumably with a move in mind. Sixteen-year-old Bess was left in charge of the family home and farm—called Corey Farm—in Marne, including the care of her brothers and sister.

Corey Farm's neighbors came close to being a microcosm of recent immigration into the state, and the names of all of them appear in Bess's letters. All were farmers belonging either to the first or, more commonly, to the second wave of pioneering settlers, the same generation as Edwin Corey and Margaret Brown, both of whom sprang from English stock. Lands to the north were worked by another Englishman, Mason Fish, who farmed with his sons E. F. Fish and George M. Fish. Across the road to the east were the families of E. A. Noon and Samuel Line; the Noons shared mailbox space with the Coreys at a crossroads. A near neighbor to the east was Benjamin J. Harris; his daughter Valerie was one of Bess Corey's closest girlhood friends and long-time correspondents. John Lamer's farm lay a mile and a half to the north; on his property stood another of Clay Township's rural schools. The Ed Armstrong family, in whose lives young Bess took an active interest, farmed directly to the north, and M. A. Mutum, whose son George would later marry Valerie Harris, was located not much farther to the northwest, just across the town line into Monroe Township. Fritz Schief (Bess spells it Scheef), a member of the large and industrious German contingent in Shelby and Pottawattamie Counties, farmed rich land a mile to the northeast of Coreys and early on emerged as one of the most successful and admired men of the area. Even while disruptive anti-German sentiments tore at the social fabric during World War I, the big, new, four-square Schief home was pointed out with pride, and its photograph was prominently displayed when a thick volume of county history appeared in 1915.

| 1

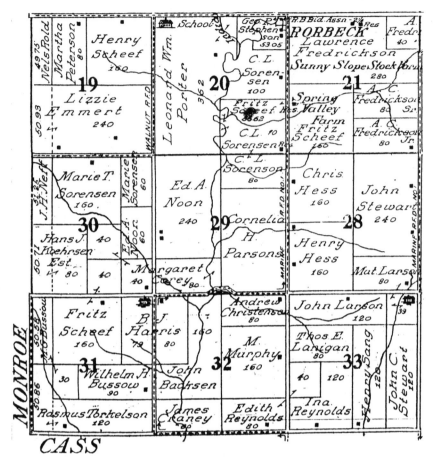

1911 plat map of Clay Township showing the location of the Corey farm. Bridging the bottom of sections 29 and 30 is Margaret Corey's name, along many of the neighbors' names that Bess mentions in her letters: Noons, Scheefs, Harrises, Stewarts, etc. There are at least three icons showing schools in the area close enough for Bess to have taught there. From *Atlas of Shelby County, Iowa, Containing Maps of the Townships of the County.*

(opposite) Valerie Harris, 1906, age sixteen.
From a photograph donated by Carol Mutum Sampson
to the Walnut Historical Museum.

Bess's mother, Margaret Brown Corey.

(opposite)

Bess's father, Edwin O. Corey, on the right, with his brothers John (center) and Frank (left).

Several Irishmen—and some Scots-Irish—lived in the area. In addition to the Noons, John C. Stewart farmed an area in Harlan east of the Corey Farm. Bess's connection with the Stewart family would prove valuable when in 1905 she would need a boarding place while she attended a teacher's institute in her attempt to gain a qualifying certificate to teach rural school. Patrick Murphy farmed in the same area. Another Irishman, Thomas E. Lanigan—his daughter Mary, along with Valerie Harris, was an especially dear friend to Bess— worked land between the Noons and the Stewarts.

Close to the northeast was the farm property of the Sorensens, Danish settlers, whose daughters Inger and Sena Bess knew well. Many Danish immigrants were concentrated at Elk Horn, just into Audubon Township, as well as in Shelby's Harlan area and in Polk Township, where Bess taught in 1908. With the presence of the English, the Irish, the Germans, and the Danes, the Corey neighborhood could be described as representative, a melting pot—perhaps more accurately described as a Mulligan stew—of new Americanism.

A number of family relatives also lived close by. Atlantic, the largest town in the area, with a population in 1900 of more than five thousand, was the seat of Cass County, and had become something of an enclave for Edwin Corey's siblings. His bachelor brother John resided in Atlantic, as well as his sisters Mary, Hattie, and Rachel ("Aunt Rate" to Bess), who also remained unmarried. Their sister Jennie Corey, a teacher, had come to Iowa and married James D. Dunlavy, a former superintendent of a county school system. After Ed's father, Jeremiah, died in 1896, his widow, Anna Mariah ("Grandma Corey"), made her home in Atlantic also. Until her death in 1912, she acted as a stabilizing influence in Bess's life. All of these relatives would have been within the circle of people Bess visited, wrote to, and at various times depended upon.

The Corey children in September, 1902. Back row (l-r), Olney, Fuller, Bess. Front row (l-r), Rob, Ethel, Challenge. Missing is Paul, who was not born until 1903.

* *

OCTOBER 10, 1904

Mamma & Papa:

We are all right but very busy with little time to write

The boys[1] are doing fine so far and we have had lots of visitors

I churned wednesday, baked bread on thursday and had one visitor, ironed on friday & the boys had three visitors in the evening, I churned, baked and made pickels on saturday We had twelve visitors yesterday and it rained last night and this morning

The thrashers got to Noons[2] saturday afternoon but haven't thrashed there yet

I am baking bread to day but not washing

The boys haven't finished the plowing but are doing about as well as they can will close in haste and get this mailed

could write enough to fill a book if I had time[3]

Bess F. Corey

[written in the top margin of page 2 of the letter, presumably in the handwriting of her mother, Margaret: "written to us when at West Plains Mo."]

1. "The boys" are Bess's brothers: James Olney (called "Olney" or "Bid"), 18; Henry Fuller (called "Fuller," "Toad," or "Toadie"), 15; Robert Longfellow ("Rob"), 10; Challenge Richard ("Chall"), 4; and Paul Frederick ("Paulie"), 1. Bess doesn't mention her sister Gertrude Ethel ("Ethel"), 8, in this particular letter (CMW).

2. Probably the William Noon family, mentioned in *Bachelor Bess*, p. 425, as being neighbors of the Coreys (CMW).

3. A common expression of Bess's, who needed only the right occasion to expound at length upon any topic.

Walnut

Around November, 1904, Bess entered the Walnut School, about seven or eight miles west of Corey Farm. Built in 1875, this two-story building housed a "graded school," in which Bess could qualify to teach if she could pass both her coursework and then the teaching certification examinations. She boarded at the William Copley home, working for at least part of her keep. According to the federal census of 1900, members of the Copley family included William and his wife (her name is illegible on the census) and their grown children William, Irma, Helen, and Mary.

The small, railroad town of Walnut had a large number of German families, many of whose children were Bess's classmates.

The Walnut School where Bess first set her sights on a teaching career. This school burned in 1913, so the photograph was taken sometime before that. Original in Walnut Historical Museum.

Classroom in the Walnut school, ca. 1904–1905. It is not known if Bess is in the photograph, although many of the classmates she mentions are identified. Front row, from bottom of the picture to the top: Cardie Wolf Walter, Glen Carey, Leo Stuart, Grace Staman Hammond, Amanda Koeppe, Martha Mueller, Kate Burke Eagan. Other people in the picture, although their placement is not identified: Laura Eroe Furey, Floyd Thompson, Mildred Bloom Riddle, Grace Koeppe, Alice Galvin Craig, Georgie Bunton, Harriet Spangler Hector, Grace Mix Harris, Theo Carey, Harry Hector, Alta Mick, Edmond Moeller, and Superintendent Van Meter. Original in Walnut Historical Museum.

NOVEMBER 30, 1904 WALNUT, IOWA

Dear Ma and the rest:

Well, I'm getting started alright but I would like to have pa send me some more money because today when the Principal called the tuition pupils up to get their *yaller* slips I found that the tuition must be paid by the term (3 months) in advance I heard one of the others ask if they couldn't pay part of it at a time and he said no they did n't want to be bothered with it and if possible to pay it today or tomorrow

I haven't enough and I would rather not borrow unless I have to

I got some of my books second-hand of Lauretta Chambles and some of them I got new, the Grammers are *so* different from those we used out in the country. they are n't started in physiology yet. and we have Merrils Slant writting and the same kind of drawing books the children have out there use

Miss L.___[1] the 8th grad[e] teacher gives about 35 min. home work. and all the Algebra will be home work to and I will have about 70 pages to catch up but I guess I'll make it all right.

I think I will try to mail you a letter every Friday morning after this so you will get it Saturday and if you don't get time to write me a little Sundays you wont any time.

Tell the boys I've had to *set in* every day so far, and there are seven tuition pupil in the 8th grade and Alfred Rasmusen sets right behind me and tell Olney it was awful smart of him to hide that quarterly so I couldn't find it.

And today I was sent up to the principal and I have to go up stair right after first recess and recite Algebra and this morning was the first time I tried it and the teacher asked one of the girls what division was and she said she *didn't know* and after asking two or three she gave them a little lecture on being in the 9th grade and not knowing that much even and then she asked if any one could tell and for a wonder I could and every one in the room *turned to rubber*. Of course they turned when the teacher spoke

Well I guess I will close hoping to hear from you soon I remain
Your daughter
Elisabeth[2] F Corey
P.S. We had fire drill this morning not even the teacher was expecting it and she was reading aloud when she heard it, we all marched

out across the school yard to a certain tree and then marched back and one boy got a black mark for *communicating*.

Do you think pa has a good fresh cow for sale or have you Mr. Copley is talking of buying one

1. Miss Leonard.

2. In these early letters, Bess spelled her name using the "s" rather than the "z" she used in her homesteading letters (CMW).

. . . .

DECEMBER 8, 1904 WALNUT, IOWA

To Mrs. E. O. Corey, Marne, Iowa

Dear Mamma: —

I received your letter and that check alright and am much obliged for the later. It was enough to pay my debts and some over but I've got to get some more things yet so it wont last long I'm afraid

Please hurry up that under skirt and stockings for these are the darnedest darned[1] socks I ever owned I guess when I go down to mail this letter I'll buy a pair and charge it up.

There are two more new pupils in our room. John Eggerstodt & Ernest Feldhahn and John looks so much like the pictures of Sunny Jim that the girls call him that. and Ernest [is] tall good looking serious and stylish from his barber cut hair to his patent leather shoes. they are such a contrast.

We are all expected to keep our seats while in the school-room and should not communicate without permission The other day the girl ahead of me said "Miss Leonard you want to watch them." (Alfred and I) Miss Leonard said why & Perle said "she turns around." I said Perle don't you ever turn around? She turned around and looked me square in the face and said *she didn't turn around* and Miss Leonard asked her what she was doing then and oh how the rest laughed

I don't come home for my dinner any more, it was too much sugar for a cent, so I just take an apple or two. I keep the teachers chair warm, while she goes for her dinner, and talk to the boys while they eat theirs.

The dress maker came home with Irma Friday and went away this evening. We havent washed this week we have been so busy.

Ida Copley stayed over Sunday night with us and we, Irma, Mary, Ella, Ida and I went to hear Rev. Mr Barker, the evangelest

He asked for all the church members to stand and as Mary said afterward she was so glad he called for the church members and not for the christians to stand

Rev Barker addressed the school Mon. morning and gave us a splended talk

Alfred, says Harry Smith is in Omaha he don't know whether he is going to school or not

Clarence Brown just stoped going to school the week before I comensed he was in the 8th to.

I and Lauretta Chamblis met Mrs. Dave Kite as we were going to school one morning she asked if I were staying in town now and the next morning as I passed she came out and went down the walk to the store house and she called and asked me where I was staying and how you were.

Little Helen has slept with me several nights and can get along without her Auntys first rate if I tell her about the Little Pigs

Tonight her grandma found a caterpillar cralling on her neck and after I brushed it off she said "Grandma my but you made a fuss about that"

Well it is half after eleven so I will close hoping to hear from you and the rest soon

I remain your daughter

Elisabeth F. Corey

Our teacher is just lovely.

[written in the top margin of the first page:] Which of the boys help you in the house? What is O doing now? How does Fuller like the teacher? How is your work coming on? I haven't been to bed before ten since the first night I came

1. "Darndest darned" is an example of Bess's compulsive punning.

DECEMBER 16, 1904 WALNUT, IOWA

To Mrs. E. O. Corey

Dear Ma and the rest: —

Please excuse paper and pencil for I didn't write last night
Those thing came late but will do for another time.

Little Helen informed her grandpa last night at supper that they
didn't have to fold up their hands out to Ed Corey's[1] that most killed
Mary and Irma off.

Professor Brown State inspector of High Schools and he inspected
things in great shape

How many rabbits have they got this winter so far

That letter was not an invitation it was mostly questions and O so
nice You can send some one after me a week from this evening or a
week from tomorrow

Will close your daughter

Elisabeth F. Corey

1. Apparently the Coreys did not say a formal grace at meals.

JANUARY 10, 1905 WALNUT, IOWA

To Mrs. E. O. Corey

Dear Ma and the rest: —

I received my repoart card this evening and Mrs. Copley as my
guardean signed it so I can take it back in the morning.

Miss Flora has nearly completed her writing but needs a fue more
bright ideas and if you can mail her those other to Year Books she will
return them to me and make it all right about the postage and her
address is *Miss Flora Koeppe* She would like to get the books befor
Saturday as that is the only time she has to work on it.

Tell Olney, a boy here asked me if I had a brother married and I
had a chance to tell him as he told the peddler that I didn't but I had
one that was going to be

I'm up with the rest in algebra

One of the boys said Bessie Kahr, I guess that is the way you spell it, said she knew me by the name of Bessie and she didn't know my name was Elisabeth.

I guess Ive got my accounts straight now

I started this last night and came down town this noon and got Mr Bruce to tell me the price of those things I guess I better close now and go back to the schoolhouse I enclose my grades and account

And remain

Elisabeth F. Corey

[Enclosure: Bess's grades]

Deportment E

Studentship E

Spelling 90

Reading 95

Writing 92

Aritmetic 85

Grammar 80

U. S. History 93

Music 90

[Enclosure: Bess's record of expenses]

tuition	$ 8.00
Grammar	.25
Arithmetic	.30
Algebra	.55
Speller	.20
2 scratch tablets	.10
2 erasers	.10
ink	.05
copybook	.10
drawing book	.15
music note book	.15
composition book	.05
	$10.00
Bible	2.25
Stamps	.20
[postal] cards	.05
	$12.50

To Mrs. E. O. Corey

Dear Ma and the rest: —

Mr. C mailed my card in the forenoon and Olney mailed your letter in the afternoon. I don't see how on earth you kept the schoolma'am[1] over night as close for room as you are but your speaking of it made me think of something although perhaps I aught not to mention it. It is in connection with the social. Of couse I would be jolly glad to have O— come after me Feb 10th and if you were not so crowded I would fetch another girl along. She hasnt any brothers and so dosen't get to go as much as she might. her folks are renters and she is such a jolly, nice kind of girl, she would put up with any thing and think it was alright, it would be a great treat to her and all the rest of us.

Are Mr & Mrs. Armstrong back and house keeping? that reminds me of something, Ida Copley was in today and Reba and her little sister were over. Reba was telling that she received a letter the other day from a *Fern Armstrong* cordially inviting her to come and visit her in her new home, she couldn't guess who on earth it was from, at first, but as she only knew of one Fern, she thought it must be that Fern Line was married but she couldn't see what she was writing to her for I told her of the wedding and ask her if Fern had much to say. She said no it didn't amount to much only that Mr and Mrs Sorensen were away and she would be so pleased to have her (Reba) come and spend a week with her in her new home and some of them would be in town soon. Now it struck me that Fern ask me about Reba last New Years eve and why on earth does she want to stir up an acquaintance with Reba Copley unless it is to find out a fue interesting things about others.

Uncle Charlie wants Reba to take teachers examination this spring and I guess we will take it together which will be much better than alone, we will work up together and with hints from Ida I hope to get through but it is doubtful. Ida says "Sign your name McCorey or OCorey and he will think you are Irish and you will get a certificate even if you don't know beans" she says that a "pull" or a $10 bill will fetch a certificate quicker than brains.

Miss Leonard came to me Friday noon and said she and Gertrude Backus[2] had planed to come out to see me that evening but she had just got word that they were going to have company that evening so she couldn't come and for me to get my things and come over to dinner with her she had sent word to her sister that I was coming so I went and she and Gertie are coming next Friday if nothing happens.

We had it 26° below last week and we had to have some of our exercise and running in the middle of the forenoon to get our feet warm.

I'm anxious to know how the Creamry meeting came out.

I would like to have a Grammar a Physiology and a Civil Goverment or two

I've 65¢ and have got to get some stamps and envelopes which will take 25 or 30 cents Say if you can find a Nonpariel[3] that came the last week in Dec. that has a list of the curent events of the past year I wish you would save it fore me I need it in my business.

Will Murphey's wedding in the Catholic church here was a swell affair I've heard, his bro. Father Murphey married them

I suppose if Wheelers were over you have heard all about that Turner girls wedding. you know that Mr. Jacobsen that used to work at Scheefs,[4] that Edwin Armstrong knew at Ames well he was to the wedding, and I am acquainted with his sister and she told me about it.

I lost a book last week, with my name in it and one of her brothers found it and sent it to me.

Mrs and Mr. Backus are to start for Dakota tomorrow but George ain't going isn't that jolly.

I must close it is getting so late so please write soon, yours,
Elisabeth F. Corey
[written at the top of the last page:] If you haven't used those wollen stockings please send them to me if you get a chance

1. Often a snowstorm would make it unsafe for a teacher to attempt to reach her boarding place. The Coreys seem to have offered shelter to the teacher at School #9, close to Corey Farm.

2. An interesting story about Gertrude Backus contained in Roma Arndt's *Walnut Memoirs* (p. 84) is that she was "the first woman to drive through Yellowstone Park, and hers was the second car to drive through" (CMW).

3. The *Nonpareil* was the weekly newspaper from nearby Council Bluffs.

4. May refer to Emma and Henry Schief (or Scheef), who lived one-half a mile west of Corey Farm.

To Mrs. E. O. Corey

Dear Ma

I got your card but did not get the legging because G. & H. didn't have a pair of Ladies leggings in the store and so I went to Madsen's[1] and they didn't have any eather I was only out of school one day with the grippe[2] but Mrs. C. is having it pretty bad at present I washed yesterday and we dried the clothes in the house, I've been helping withe the milking night and morning and to night the lantern went out and I couldn't see wether I was milking in the pail or in the dark.

How was the social Friday I wanted to go so bad that I was as blue as the monkey who got the first dip but the wether being so bad and Mrs. C. being sick the next day I guess its a mighty good thing I didn't go.

Mr Copleys horse isn't much better and he has been up with her so much he is about played out, he went down after more medecine about twelve oclock last night and the snow was waist deep here[3] in the hollow and he could hardly get through. he didn't attempt to haul milk to day. I wounder how on earth I'll get to school tomorrow

Will's have a new boy and Amanda has been awful sick. Mack brought up a letter this evening to say she was some better

Could Olney read my card? I wrote it at school and the children were having a high old time they up set my ink, and then before I got it finished Colman saw a sleigh comming so I just put my tag to it and let him have it.

I am going to Avoca Friday to take the examination. and hope to pass though it seems to be a hope against fate but I am working and trusting and I hope you can send me some money so I wont have to borrow.

You may not hear from me again till after it is over but I must close for it is getting late and I want to try some soap and water for my complexion

E. F. C.

Monday forenoon Feb 13. The drifts are so bad that I had to give up going to school and we didn't get throug milking till ten minutes to nine Mr Charlie Copley and Bert came up to help Mr C. build a frame for that sick horse they came around through a field to avoid the drifts and then they got in some bad ones.

Mrs Copley is better and is going to have them mail some letters for her when they go back so I thought I would write a little more and send this

I have books here and can study to better advantage than at school so am not missing so much

E. F. C.

Well I've thought of something more and so will open my letter and put it in

Do you think it would be alright to give my age 18? One *person* advised me to as a little white lie like that wouldn't hurt me or any one else and I wouldn't stand any show if I didn't and Mrs. Copley says any one would take me to be twenty any way and few would doubt my being twenty-two (a compliment to my youth and beauty) I'm passed seventeen so I've a notion to try it if you think it will be alright

Laura Halloway sent word that she would be at the train to meet me if possible and for me to come to their house and stay

I hope you will get this tomorrow so will close and get at that book
Yours with love,
Elisabeth F. Corey

1. G. & H. and Madsen's were dry goods stores in Walnut.

2. Another name for influenza.

3. The *Shelby County Republican* reported on February 16, 1905, that the county was receiving its "heaviest snow for years," declaring "33 inches so far and no melt. Trains blocked, coal running out" (CMW).

. . . .

FEBRUARY 18, 1905 WALNUT, IOWA

To Mr. & Mrs. E. O. Corey
Dear Pa and Ma and the rest:

Well I went to Avoca as I said I would And Oh my what a time— well maybe I better begin at the beginning.

You know what kind of weather we had about a week ago well last Monday the 13th, there was four or five feet deep of snow and in the evening I went up to Koeppe's and went to the Contest with them we went around south, as the Koeppe Boys had made a path for the girls to go to school, that way.

The speaking was alright but there wasn't many pleased with the way the honors were given. Minnie Cissna won the gold medal everyone thought that was allright But everyone thought that Harry Hecter aught to have had the honors ahead of Glen Carey and that Edmond Burke should have had the honor ahead of Grace Mick.

There was one girl who sang a German song, or was to rather, she did sing at the preliminary contest and did fine but when she came on the stage Monday she seemed to be alright but at the end of the first verse she stoped in the middle of a word and her head fell forward on her breast and then she turned and walked off the stage and before she got out of sight she fell in a dead faint I haven't heard from her since.

Well after the contest I lost sight of the Koeppe girls and as Mr Copley had finished diging out a path from the corner of the pasture so we could get through I came back the shorter way with Ellen Frisby and the Chamblises. we all went in to the Hardware store to get warm before we started home and I told Eddie (Don't you tell the boys that it was all hokus pokus about his name being Edward and that his real name is Eddie or I will never hear the last of it) I was going to hunt the path he dug for me (He and I had a little talk the Friday before. we were both in snow up to our knees and he said he would dig me a path if I would just give him time) well I got through alright and the next morning there was such a blizzard we couldn't see the cribb and I gave up going to school that day and Wednesday Mr Copley Telephoned for Bert Copley and some other men to come and dig out the road and they got it finished just before noon. I tried to go to school by going around by Koeppes but when I got into snow four inches above my knees I pulled out and came back. I got through the east way at noon and that is all I've been to school this week for I spent Thursday forenoon in getting ready to go to Avoca. I went Thursday afternoon for the trains are so irregular I didn't dare risk puting it off till Friday morning. I got to Avoca about four or a little after Laura was not there but I saw her comming down the street at almost a trot.

You know she wrote for me to come there and stay at her house. she pressed me to come and see her when she was here, well they all

Amelia, Ada, Flora, Grace, and Amanda Koeppe, in Avoca, Iowa.
Original in Walnut Historical Museum.

did what they could to make it pleasant for me and refused positively to take any pay for it. I didn't

to be continued in our next.

Feb 19. [switches to pencil from pen here; obviously written at a different time] feel hardly right about it but Laura acted hurt at my suggesting pay so I had to let it go and it only cost me $1.39 and I had borrowed a V[1] from Mr. Copley. so I had plenty of money

The train was late Friday morning so Mr McManus was late and I dont think we got started to writting till half after ten and then we had to stop early as it got so cold and when Saturday night came I had only finished eight branches and had to hurry to catch my train I will have to go to Oakland four weeks from now and take the other two branches I think I made good grades in two or three branches and will pass in two or three and am doubtful about the rest but I can find out and by paying an extra fea can take them over of course

I didn't have the gritt to give my age eighteen and Friday when I paid my dollar he asked my age, and it took all the nerve I had to answer that I was not eighteen yet. he said "Oh yes I see you put it eighteen in Nov. in the preliminarys" and I said "Then I couldnt hold a certificate?" he thought a little bit and said "not hardly we wouldn't hesitate at a month or so but that is quite a while, but of course some are more mature at that age than others and you will do better than the majority if you pass the examinations. and if you do we will settle the question of age then." I think he will give me a permit if I pass so I will study like the dickens for three or four weeks and make another try I came off in such a rush that I forgot my mail.

As the train pulled into Walnut a man with two suit cases and a valice brushed passed me and got off befor the train had hardly stopped. I looked after him and thought he was in a mighty big rush and when I got up town I passed him talking to a girl on the street corner and thought he had got over his rush all of a suddent. I went on a few blocks and heard Frank Ware say "Hello Bill" to someone behind me but thought nothing of it till I got passed Chamblises and turned to see the man with the suit cases following me and then I turned around and said Good evening Mr. Copley, and we waded the snowdrifts together. he went this afternoon on the three o'clock. I tell you what he is a regular dandy he scooped some pathes for us and brought in coal and gave me an awful dandy new penholder and some new pens

I read your letters last night and was real glad to get them thoug I didn't get the check I expected but I suppose you didn't open my letter before you sent it.

I'm awful sorry about that social but It realy couldn't be helped I supose and if the boys could have seen me take the train they would have forgotten there ever was a social.

Of course I could not take teachers examination in those short skirts and Mrs Copleys were as large for me as mine were for Sena Nelson so I borrowed one of Ellen Frisbie you need not look shocked for it was just a fit, one of those kind that are big around the bottom and it just cleared the floor.

I did up my white waist and with my swell hat I assure you I just looked stunning I realy felt quite vain

Mrs Copley is much better but kind of shakey in the knees. and I still help with the milking and must change my dress and go at it pretty soon and I've got another letter to write this evening to.

Say I believe I'm going down & get me a couple of pair of stockings I've only got two pair with feet to 'em and I put four big patches on the best pair to wear to Avoca I'm out of darning cotton and those short ones are not warm enough for winter as I have no leggings but those short ones Mrs Copley gave me

There is plenty more to write but I can't afford the postage.

You better all write next time if you don't write oftener. will close and remain as ever

Elisabeth F Corey

Hurry up that check.

1. Roman numeral for 5, so it is assumed that she means a $5 bill (CMW).

• •

FEBRUARY 21, 1905 WALNUT, IOWA

To Mrs. E. O. Corey

Dear Ma and the rest.—

I received your note and check this evening after school will cash the check tomorrow and pay up

I suppose you have received my letter of the 18th and 19th before this and hope papa will be much better when this reaches you[1]

When I was up to Avoca taking that examination I saw a girl there that looked like the Smart girls well it seems that Genevera and Tom Smart were taking the exams and for some reason or other Genevera ask some one who I was and Mary Backus or Elsie Linfor told her and she told the girls and Monday morning when I got to school I found that the whole town knew and were ready to ask if I thought I would pass. I got a letter from Valerie[2] last night she wants me to come up and go [to] the masquerade ball at Rohrbeck next Saturday night.

Well I guess this is all you'll have time to read so I will enclose my account and close remaining as ever your daughter

Elisabeth F Corey

[Enclosure: Bess's financial account]

Account of Elisabeth F. Corey

$1.02 cash on hand Jan 9.

side combs	.25
writing paper	.05

$1.02 - .30 = $.72 cash on hand Jan 11.

scratch paper	.10
envelopes	.10
[postal] cards	.05
stamps	.15
book	.10

$.72 - .50 = $.22 cash on hand Jan 31

$5.00 borrowed- - Check $5.00, paid Feb 22

$5.22 cash on hand

Ticket for contest	.25
Car fare	.19
Examination fee	1.00
Car fare	.20
Stockings 2 pair	.30
Handkerchiefs	.30

$5.22 - 2.24 = $2.98 cash on hand Feb. 21

1. The first indication of Mr. Corey's illness from the pneumonia that will soon take his life (PG). The *Shelby County Republican* mentioned in its obituary that "he had been complaining for a couple of weeks, but went to town five days before his death to get medicine. He took to his bed only three days before he passed away" (CMW).

2. Valerie Harris, oldest daughter of Ben Harris, friend of the Corey family.

Harlan

SHELBY COUNTY, IOWA

JUNE 1905 TO AUGUST 1905

The sons of the James Stewart family, ca. late 1890s to early 1900s. Back (l-r), Samuel, Isaiah, George, Andrew, Thomas. Front (l-r), John, Richard, Joseph.

After the sudden death of her father in late February, Bess had to leave school to help her family get through the hard times that followed. In June she was able to go to Harlan, the county seat of Shelby County, to attend six weeks of summer school in hopes of gaining at least a temporary teaching certificate so she could make enough money to help her family financially. The *Shelby County Republican* reported on June 8, 1905, that the teachers would be Allan Peterson of Randolph, V. J. Robinson of Brayton, and W. J. Luxford of Kirkman, and that G. A. Luxford would be the superintendent. The school advertised that it would teach "all branches" and that exams would be "given at the end of summer school for teaching certification." There was also to be a "normal" (teacher's) institute that summer, with teachers from Chicago and Iowa City—but Bess was not yet qualified for that.

Harlan was the closest thing to a city in the whole of Shelby County. It was here that the Shelby County Breeders' Association owned a splendid sales pavilion on the county fairgrounds, where the best breeding stock was bought and sold. If the name of Harlan was known nationally at all, it was for Charles Escher and Son's experimentation with the black Aberdeen Angus cattle imported from Scotland. In 1902 the Eschers were the pride of Shelby County; their cattle had won the grand championship at the Chicago International Exposition. The Eschers' great spread, Lincoln Ranch, at the southwestern edge of Harlan, was furnished with all the modern conveniences, including one of the first telephones to have long-distance capability.

While in Harlan, Bess boarded with a family in the large clan of Irish descendants by the name of Stewart (or Stuart, as she spells it here), but trying to discover which household she actually lived in is difficult. Phil Gerber stated that Bess lived at 1001 10th Street but does not list his source for that information. Regardless, most of the various Stuart/Stewart families listed in Shelby County in the 1905 Iowa State Census seem to have been related, if one can judge by how frequently Bess mentions that they are visiting one another.

Sarah is the person she mentions most often in this set of letters, and her first letter mentions "Mr. George," so she probably had a room in the George E. Stewart household listed in the 1905 state census with Anna and Sarah C. Stewart (no relationships given in this census). The "Mr. and Mrs. Sam Stuart" she mentions are

Sam R. and Emma A. Stewart living in Walnut. In the nearby hamlet of Jacksonville, there was an Andrew, Richard, and "One" Stewart ("One" seemingly the census-taker's shorthand for someone whose name he couldn't remember or didn't get, for there is a One Peterson, a One Nielsen, a One Christensen, and a One Bremer in various other families; and that is just a single page of the 45-page census list for the Harlan area.) The Charlie Stewart she mentions is likely the Charles W. living with David W., Dollie M., Donald B., and Alice M. Stewart in Harlan.

JUNE 26, 1905 HARLAN, IOWA

To Mrs. E. O. Corey

Dear ma:—

Summer school	$6
Institute	1
Examination	1
Board	23.50
Expence Total	$31.50

I am taking eight branches[1] and we recite in the forenoon. I got me a new hand bag with two inner pockets, and small coin purse for .75

I cant get me a ready made waist I tried several places and they havent any large enough only in white and those are so thin.

I can make these do though by washing my white one.

I can do it my self which will save expence.

I have an east room with two windows, bereau with large mirear, marble toped wash stand a closet to hang my clothes in a feather bed and springs to sleap on and a straight backed chair and a rocker and may not have to share my room with anyone

Stuarts seem to have lots of company. I went to bed early last night and did nont meet Mr George or Andrew Stuart till this morning.

Will mail this, this afternoon and get me a couple of books. Please send me some money soon for Mr Luxford said I could pay today or tomorrow.

Good bye

Elisabeth Corey

[on an enclosed scrap of paper:] I am going to open my letter and add a note.

Have you heard of the terrible accident at Jas McMahans? I've just heard the whole thing. the child was resting better last night but they say it will be a blessing if he doesn't live.

[written above the inside address, probably added after the complete letter written:] If Miss Armstrong knew how well acquainted I was getting with *some* folks there would be a wailing and gnashing of teeth.

1. "Branches" would be roughly equivalent to "classes" or "subjects." Edward White's chapter on education in his 1915 *Past and Present of Shelby County, Iowa*

(p. 420) states that the branches taught at the normal institute were "English, grammar, history of education, American literature, didactics, natural philosophy, astronomy, arithmetic, reading, vocal music, geography, United States history, physiology, orthography, civil government, and algebra" (CMW).

. . . .

JULY 1, 1905 HARLAN, IOWA

To Mrs. E. O. Corey

Dear Ma,—

I received your letter and check Thursday evening. Well I'm through one week of Summer School and like it, but its hard work this reciting from 7:30 till noon and then studyind till suppertime and sometimes after.

That accident at Jas McMahan's happened last Saturday evening. The little boy who is about four years old threw a stick and hit a horse that was running loose and the horse kicked him in the face breaking his nose and both cheek bones and knocked out one eye. Drs. Hanna and McClees could do nothing for him and at eleven oclock that night they took him to the Atlantic hospital. Mrs Duhnan was here and said it was like a funeral procession. They don't think he will live and say it will be a blessing if he does not live.

Miss Anthony seemed very much interested in me from the time she found that my name was Corey. She offered to lend me books and as this old Arithmetic isn't any good I've been using one of hers. Yesterday she asked me where I lived I told her and she asked if I was any relation to Jennie Corey[1] I said that I was and that I lived in southwest Clay[2] she said "Oh yes I know where the other Coreys used to live I was so well acquainted with Jennie Corey that used to be and am pleased to meet you.["]

The instructors all call me Miss Corey except Mr Robinsen and yesterday he called me Elisabeth in quite a *We're acquainted now* sort of way. I like them all but the superintendants brother. He is a good judge of human nature and an awful tease. We've been studying the bones and he passed the skull around for some of them to name the bones he then passed around some peices of decayed or honnycombed bone. and as soon as he noticed that I never touched them I knew I was in for it. Thursday he asked me to recite on a certain subject and I told quite a bit but he watched me so close I couldn't stand it so I quit and he said "Oh don't be so bashfull Miss Corey take right a hold and tell us about it I know you know more than that." I just felt like hitting him with a brick. Yesterday he brought some bones down and held them out to me so close they nearly touched my hand. I jurked my hand back and shuddered. I just couldn't help it but it tickeled him awfuly he steped back and oh how he laughed.

Did I tell you that Mr & Mrs Sam Stuart took dinner here one day this week? Mrs Stuart used to be Miss Emma Alwell whose father was down to our house with Mr. Knox.

There is a rubber tired buggy and sorrel team here. guess I'll try them one of thes days.

Must close and get to work so write when you can or have one of the boys write

Good bye

Elisabeth F Corey

Harlan Iowa

Box 461.

1. Jennie Corey, Bess's aunt, sister of Edwin O. Corey. She married James D. Dunlavy and lived with him in the hamlet of Corley at this time.

2. Clay township.

. . . .

JULY 5, 1905 HARLAN, IOWA

To Mrs. E. O. Corey

Dear ma,—

I received Grandmas letter, your note and the one dollar bill. am much obliged for the same.

Chautauqua[1] commences next Friday eve at 7:30.—as it is in the educational line Mr Luxford is anxious for all of the Summer School students [to] take it in and has secured the chance for them to get season tickets for $2 apeice when the usual price is $3 per ticket. It is to be aranged so as not to interfear with our work so I am going to take it in.

Well, this is the last day of Harlan's three days Carnival[2] and oh such a time.

I wouldn't swap the fun I had Monday night for the two funniest weeks I ever had in my life.

Monday I was so hungry for ice cream that I told Sarah that I would pay for the ice if she would make some. It only took 15 cents worth to make a gallon of ice cream.

We went down town in the evening and got some fire crackers and Sarah telephoned to her beau to come up and have some ice cream. There was just Sarah, Charlie, George and I. After we had our ice cream we shot off fire crackers and George who is a perfect clown just kept things going.

Yesterday Andrew came in and he and George went out into the country and didn't get back till this morning.

Sarah and I went down town yesterday forenoon and we met a man that I knew and he walked up with us and the first thing I knew Sarah was gone and we were walking alone. We stoped on the corner here by Stuarts and had our talk out and when I got here Sarah was calmly getting dinner as though she hadn't been away from home for a week. She insists that she had been home an hour but she must have stretched it some. I've got one of those little flags that a man gave me. I wore it all day yesterday and am going to keep it to remember the Fourth by

I went to church last Sunday evening with Sarah. after church a smiling gent. steped up with a polite good evening and walked home with us and it wasn't Sarah beau either

One day Mrs Stuart scalded her arm and put flour and a cloth on it and came in for me to tie it up. I asked her if she wanted me to treat it and she said I might as it hurt pretty bad. at supper she was telling them how my treating it stoped the pain and she started to show George the spot and was amazed to find that no trace of it was left.

I've had to depend on C. S.[3] *so much* lately. yesterday all of a sudden something got wrong with my left eye it felt stiff and I could not see out of it to speak of. Sarah said it looked blured and starey It got better after a while but the other has had a spell to day and is, you might say, unmanageable. please tell Olney to help me all he can for I fear that acording to Materia Medica that my eyes are threatening to become crossed

George says some Sunday we will go out in the country and I can talk Christian Science to that young lady who is staying at [Andrew] Stuarts There was a Mrs Henderson here the other day that Uncle Jim [Dunlavy] used to board with. she seemed pleased to make my acquaintance and invited me to call on her.

The other evening Sarah and I met Mrs Ed Fish & Mr & Mrs Charlie Fish and family in a store—Mr Fish said he recognized my picture in the sewing school picture and that it was fine & Mrs Charlie Fish invited me to come down and spend the evening some time and I guess Sarah and I will go when we get time.

I couldn't get me a white waist but finely found a store that had just got a lot of colored ones there was only one that would fit me and I got it for $1 it is medium blue with white bars and piped with white. it is quite pretty

When I get my Chautauqua ticket I will have just .45 left and no rubbers yet. my Fourth of July cost me 25 cents. Well I must close so pleas write and let me know how the corn ploughing & raspberries & black berries are

Good bye

Elisabeth F Corey

Box 461 Harlan Iowa

I inclose a note to Valerie

You know that flour sack you put in well I used that and every thing else I could get my hands on, in two days and had to go to Sarah for more. never had such a time I seemed to have cramps but didn't tell any one, just used C. S.

[written sideways on back of last page:] That is a mistake about the 45 cents for Ive got to get a book yet.

I dont need rubbers or raincoat

1. This was the heyday of the Chautauqua movement, which from its headquarters in western New York State arranged for hundreds of traveling groups to tour the nation, often holding meetings under canvas, as was the case in Harlan. The Chautauqua programs sought to balance education with inspiration and entertainment, bringing a representative blend of American culture to the hinterlands (PG).

The *Shelby County Republican* for July 13 reported that the attendance for this chautauqua was "800 in morning, 1500 afternoon, and 2500 at night" (CMW).

2. The *Shelby County Republican* reported on July 6 that the three-day carnival and celebration was "a blanket failure" because of continuous rain and muddy

streets, but that does not seem to have diminished Bess's enjoyment of the festivities (CMW).

3. The first mention of Bess's interest in Christian Science, which she followed throughout her life. She did not grow up with Christian Science. Her Episcopalian parents attended the only church in the vicinity of Corey Farm, a white Methodist Episcopal chapel across the Monroe Township line where many of the family are now buried. Here, Olney sang tenor in the choir and Fuller sometimes played his fiddle to accompany the hymns. In the community where Bess grew up, however, many denominations were represented: Catholics, Presbyterians, Congregationalists, Danish Baptists, German Lutherans, Jews, and assorted traveling preachers, revivalists, and evangelists. It was Olney who first discovered Christian Science, perhaps, as his brother Paul later suggested, in an attempt at finding a cure for his epilepsy. Bess followed Olney's lead into Christian Science, and so did their mother, Margaret. When Bess went to her various schoolteaching posts, she carried her dedication to Christian Science with her, but that did not stop her from attending whatever church or revival her friends might suggest. Neither did her enthusiasm for it prevent her from using traditional medicine on occasion. She seems to have used "healing" as a first effort, and only if that failed would she turn to a doctor for advice.

. . . .

JULY 6, 1905 HARLAN, IOWA

To J. Olney Corey, Elmdale[1]
Mr. J. O. Corey
Marne, Iowa
Dear brother

I suppose ma told you about my treating Mrs Stuart for a scalded arm. Well she has been doctering for three months for stomach trouble and has received no benifit.

This noon she said if I would not make it too expensive for her she wished I would take her case. I consented and have given her one treatment. she has stoped taking medicine and says she feels better.[2]

I will be much obliged to you for what help you can give as your understanding is perhaps greater than mine.

One beautiful thing about it is she seems to realize that it is God and my understanding of Him and not *me* that is to effect the cure.

Tonight she was all a chuckle over something and when Sarah

went out doors she said "And what do you think? Sarah says if you cure me she is going to get you to give her some treatments" so you see even skeptical Sarah is interested

Yours in haste

Elisabeth F Corey

Box 461

Harlan Ia

1. Apparently, following Edwin Corey's death, Margaret Corey began applying the name "Elmdale" to Corey Farm. Bess begins using that appellation at this point and continues to do so, sporadically (PG). The envelope is addressed this way, but the inside address is different (CMW).

2. Without training of any sort, Bess let it be known that upon request she was willing to conduct healing treatments. The specific nature of her attempts to cure illness are not discussed, but they likely followed cases and patterns written about in the *Christian Science Quarterly*, which she and Olney read whenever possible.

. . . .

JULY 12, 1905 HARLAN, IOWA

To Mr J. Olney Corey, Elmdale

Mr J Olney Corey

Marne Iowa

Dear brother,—

I received your letter yesterday noon and was both sorry and glad to get it

Was glad to hear that you had a new team. What color are they? The Chautauqua is fine and as I have a season ticket I am trying to take in all that I can and have heard twelve lectures already I had quite a long talk with Harry Westerguard yesterday and he said to tell you boys that whenever you are in Harlan to be sure and hunt him up He said for you to drive up next Sunday and see the Chautauqua out. I just wish you would, it won't cost you so very much and it will be worth much more than the cost. I would like to tell you all about it but it would take too much room.

If you come up bring me one of the large Natural Geography's. I kneed one awful bad.

I had quite a talk with Mrs Dunmore and she expressed a wish to meet mama. she gave me an Introduction to Miss Reynold's mother who said she had been looking all around for some one to give her an introduction to me.

We were excused at ten oclock to day so we could attend the lecture. Of course I went and what is more I was escorted home by Mr. Frank Crandel & he is awful nice

I wish you could have heard that noted violinest that was here. & today we had a noted singer from across the seas I think she is a Dane. The lecture last night was by Father Vauhne, a Catholic priest. The lecture was on Shakespear.

Yesterday afternoon we had "Chickens always come home to roost" by Wickersham. I will inclose a program[1] although there has been some changes in it.

George Stuarts best girl was here Sunday she is a Christian Scientist but I didn't get very well acquainted with her for she was *so busy*. She invited me out to see her

Well I must close. come Sunday if you can and don't forge[t] that Geography.

With love to all I remain

Elisabeth F. Corey

box 461

Harlan Ia

1. The program is missing from the envelope (CMW).

. . . .

JULY 21, 1905 HARLAN, IOWA

To Mrs. E. O. Corey, Elmdale

Mrs E O Corey Elmdale

Marne Iowa

Dear Ma,—

Well as you folks dont seem to care about writing to me any more I will write to you any.

I got a look at Mr. Luxfords account book the other day and was amazed to find that he hadn't given me a single X bad mark in History and all the rest had from one to five. so he isn't so bad as he seems.

I am afraid I did get a black mark today though We have been having written tests or examinations in some of the branches. We've had two in music & I got 75% & 81% the latter was above the average and the former a passing grade. I also got 95% in Arithmetic And I hope to do still better. Mr Allen Peterson, instructor in music has been trying to get us to sing more. He said if we were paying $1 a week for a room we had a right to sing all we wanted to providing it wasn't at some unearthly hour.

Last night I tried it and overheard some remarks so when he led off a string this morning I told him that I tried it and some one called and told me if I would "put that tune in a sack" that they would "carry" it for me. Mr Peterson seemed to much amused to be sympathetic for a while.

Olney took my ticket home with him I guess for I couldn't find it but Mr Yacky and George English, ticket agents, said it was all right for they knew I had a ticket alright once so I got in O.K. I went for a drink just before the lecture and found about two dozen people around the hidrent [hydrant] and when Mr Yacky saw I was waiting for a drink he went and got me one   wasn't he good.

I had a little talk with the Rev. Mr Hoyt last Monday evening.

I just received a postal from Aunt Jennie saying that J. D. steped on a pitchfork last Friday and has been in Avoca ever since having it cared for.

Sarah and I were up to Petersons one evening and Magnus lent me Garfields arithmetic so I have one I can depend on now.

I still walk to school with Frank Crandel occasionly and have had the pleasure of an introduction to Mr James Barmington. I'm ahead of Valerie one for I've met his brother also.

Write soon yours ever

Elisabeth F. Corey

. . . .

JULY 28, 1905 HARLAN, IOWA

To Mrs. E. O. Corey, Elmdale

Dear Ma,—Have just received the check and yours and Ethel's letters. am much obliged.

No I havent got the clothes brush and hope you have found it by this time

Tell Paul I'm going to pull his toes when I get home and you all can say good bye to Pat Crowe when you see me comming. I received another letter from Flora [Koeppe] last evening, she sent me the very pretty gift of a set of turn over cuffs & collar.

How is Rob's business getting along? He and Ethel both could write me if you and the big boys haven't time I suppose Rob thinks he is some punkins now he has had another birthday.

I have half a notion to go up to Fort Dodge Sunday. They have the largest bridge in the world up there. The usual price for a return ticket is between five and six dollars but Sunday you can get one for $1, and a lot of the girls are going and will take their dinners.

George [Stewart] wanted to know the other day if I would go out in the country with him Sunday but I don't know

Ethel Rink, Ida Cutshell and Nellie Green the dwarf have been to call on me this last week. I was down to call on Hazel Reynolds and received the present of a H.S.S.[1] Annual. Sarah and I was down to call on Miss Alert last evening.

We've had tests in Busines and Friendship letters and Essays this last week. The bad ones were read and criticised. Mine wasn't read I'm glad to say.

Say when you get to working so fast don't tear any of your clothes, twould be a waste of time. Why didn't you keep some of those little pinz [?] for your self as I have yours?

No I didn't write to Mrs Sorensen. I'm sorry I did not but I heard of Ingers death during Chautauqua and was doing double work and was so busy I never thought of it.

There are two men here in Harlan that I think *almost* as much of as I used to think of Chris Neerguard. One of them is Peter Kuhl. He conntrdicts my resitations ocasionly and then there is *"somethin doin"* fore a while. Its fun sometimes. I have had a hard week and will have two more of them. don't know whether I will have the courege to write again If I dont I will need a check for $10 week after next and one of the boys can meet me in Walnut Aug 13

Good Bye

Elisabeth F. Corey

[Written upside-down on top of first page of letter:] Minnie Noon is going away to school this fall. Have you heard how Willie Hildebrand is? he was no better the last I heard.

[Written sideways on back of last page of letter:] How much money was it that you gave me just before I came up here.

1. Harlan High School.

. . . .

JULY 31, 1905 HARLAN, IOWA

To Mrs. E. O. Corey

Dear Ma and the rest,—

Well I didn't go to Fort Dodge Sunday. Some of the other girls backed out and I was glad to follow the lead.

I went out to Smiths just below the County poor farm[1] for over Sunday and had a fine time.

Sunday morning we saw Mr Tom Nelson and family go past in their auto. About six oclock in the evening we heard them returning and all turned to rubber when we heard a scream and a stop. We hurried out, and up the road a ways, we saw half a dozen excited people and a mortally injured automobile. The hind axel was all to peices. They worked for about three hours to try and get it so they could bring it back to town only to have it go to peices again when they tried to move it.

It was plumb dark when they gave it up and came in the house. Mr Nelson telephoned to Mr Lana and he came out after them in his auto. Mr Nelson's mother lives the third house north of Stewarts and she said if I and some of the other girls would come over some evening, she would go down and take us through the factory. Guess I will go.

James Smith is a fine and dandy young gent. He is a good hand at farming, base-ball, foot-ball, music and talking to the girls.

He plays the piano, violin and two or three other instruments and can tease like most boys. Saturday evening Jim threw a kitten on Lida's back and then grabbed his milk pail and went to milk. I said "now s your chance." She couldn't take a dare so she caught the kitten and went out and droped it down on his back. He gave a yell and sent a stream of milk after her. She got out of the road and as I was close behind her I suffered for the sins of others.

I paid him back though and I think after this that every time he sees that spoted kitten with short tail and long toe nails he will doubtless proceed to think of *me.*

I was sitting on the porch Sunday and Smith's bee came along and saluted me on the cheek. it didn't swell though.

The piano tuner went down the street the other day trying to sooth his little son's grief by saying, "We'll take our dinner out in the woods and have a fine time" the little boy said, "Shut your mouth you old fool you, we wont either." Mr. Holly said "Oh yes we will["] and the little boy said "I told *you* to shut your mouth you old fool you, we won't either" aint that young America for you

Guess I will close so write soon Yours Ever

Elisabeth Corey

1. The county poor farm, on the southern edge of Harlan, was where destitute individuals were allowed to take up residence, often sharing farm work in exchange for their board and lodging.

. . . .

AUGUST 1, 1905 HARLAN, IOWA

To Mrs. E. O. Corey, Elmdale

Dear Ma,—

I have just been thinking that if I teach school this fall I will only have about three weeks at home after Summer School and will not have time to get the work caught up and do all the sewing up to.

Sarah Stewart is a fine dress maker and ladies tailor and she says if I get the goods she can make me a suit next week.

now if she makes it, it will fit right and be made right and in good style and if I buy a suit it will cost more and will have to be changed and then perhaps not fit right.

I enclose three samples of serviceable, stylish goods.[1] The one not marked is 43 in wide and $1 per yd the others have the price and width marked.

Think about it over night and if you see the advantage of it and can afford it send me one sample and some money. It will cost between $12 & $15 for goods, lining, trimming, & making but that isn't bad considering it on all sides.

I need a jacket worse every week.

I guess I will close for it is late and as I had a *gentleman* caller this evening I am some what behind time with my studies.

Yours as ever

Elisabeth Corey

1. These fabric samples are not with the letter (CMW).

. . . .

AUGUST 4, 1905 HARLAN, IOWA

To Mrs. E. O. Corey, Elmdale

Dear Ma,—

I received your letter this forenoon was glad to get it but disapointed because you had not rec'd my last letter yet as I was anxious to hear about that suit.

Aunt Jen was here a few minutes this noon and she said that Paulie had been very sick and you had been having a doctor for him.

I suppose I aught to have kept my mouth shut but of course I didn't. I said I guessed she must be mistaken for I had just received a letter from you and you said nothing about it. She said you must be keeping it from me to keep me from worrying. I said I thought she was mistaken. She said she wasn't that she got word from Atlantic.

I suppose the new team *was* a great supprise to Uncle John although I wrote them about it right after I heard. I guess my letter must have been quite a jar for they haven't answered it yet in spite of their worrying to hear from you.

Grandma went on to a great length in her last letter and when I wrote to her I told her that you *were* having a busy time of it but you would get through alright if people let you mind your own business.

We have had examinations in Arithmetic Grammar History and Geography today and will have the rest tomorrow.

Examinations make every one so friendly. Some who I have never met pass me with a nod and smile while others stop to ask how I think I stand and wish me all kinds of good luck and success

Mr Robinson was very kind he stoped to talk to me in the hall after I finished Arithmetic and told me all the answers he could remember so I could tell wether I got them right or not.

Tonight I just felt like flying to pieces so I went down town. I treated then another girl treated then we met a gentleman who treated and when I got home I was a pretty well treated girl. Oh yes and I had a ride to though not a very long one. I had three callers evening before last.

The other day Nora Croft, a girl I am acquainted with ask the girl who sat with her how old she thought I was and the other girl said I looked to be about fifteen but from the way I walked she should judge I was about eighty. Nora pushed her out of the seat and asked me how old I thought she was and I said she looked to be about eighty but from her actions I should judge she was about three or four. The other girl said well what *do* you think of me anyway. I told her I thought she had a good deal of brass. The rest laughed and told her it was good enough.

We don't have to write our exams with ink up here. Out of 90 who were examined in Arith 37 failed and I don't know yet wether I got through or not. Think so though.

I was over to McCords to use their phone yesterday afternoon and noticed in their parlor a case as large as a book case full of stuffed birds on branches and in nests. I'm going over with Sarah some evening and may get to know something more about them.

Will close and study orthography so

Good bye from

Elisabeth Corey

. . . .

AUGUST 5, 1905 HARLAN, IOWA

To Mrs. E. O. Corey

Dear Ma,—

Received your letter this noon am much o[b]liged for the money. I have finished the exam's am quite sure I have failed in orthography will have to study up and take it over at the end of the month. I will know how I stand in every thing Monday.

This has been dreadful weather for exams it was 102° in the shade yesterday and worse today. Sarah is down town and I am going down to get the goods for my suit. I am in a hurry for I want to catch Sarah will close for now and write more later so

Good bye from

Elisabeth Corey

AUGUST 7, 1905 HARLAN, IOWA

To Mrs. E. O. Corey

Dear Ma,—

You need not kill the fated calf in honor of my return home althoug[h] I passed the exam's and hold a certificate for three months which is better than failing in every solitary branch as some did.

I asked Mr Luxford this morning how many branches I failed in and he said "Oh about fifty." I said, "Well I failed didn't I?" I was so sure that I went down in orthography Mr. Luxford said, "No, Miss Corey, *I think* you did pretty well." and that made me feel pretty good. I guess it is comparativly good when you count all the failures. I was to a little party Saturday evening and had all kinds of fun there were twice as many girls as there were *gentlemen* and for all that I took care of two gentlemen. I invaribly quarreled with one and, the other, his brother, invaribly agreed with me.

We had ice cream, fruit, cake, and popcorn for refreshments.

I had the pleasure of meeting Miss Brown and her *friend* Mr Black at the party and when Mr Black called me "Miss Copley" it hit my funny bone pretty hard. I'm going to tell Miss Irma that folk mistake me for her. We are so much alike any way you know. I am enjoying Institute very much.

The other day a lady came to me and ask if I didn't take the examination in Avoca last Spring. I said I took part of it. She said she thought she saw me—and that she was one of the seniors in the high school then. She asked if my name was not Corey and if I lived near Marne and knew Sorensens I said yes and she said her name was Loi and she is a cousin of Inger and Sena Sorensen and while visiting there heard them speak so often of Bessie Corey.

She said her Uncle had promised her the school for next year if she passed but she failed in four branches. Of course she can take the exam at the end of the month but may not pass. just out of High School she does not stand an extra show for I don't think she attended Summer School any where. Better not tell the children though.

Must close and go down town after basting thread so

Good bye from

Elisabeth F. Corey

Harlan, Iowa

AUGUST 8, 1905 HARLAN, IOWA

To Mrs. E. O. Corey, Elmdale

Dear Mother,—

I have received your letter and it was almost more than I could stand. I always felt as though I would rather do any thing rather than teach school but I thought you wanted me to and you were so dissapointed in my failing last spring that I made up my mind I would go on and make a teacher of myself and teach one year if I never did anything else as long as I lived.

It was awful hard to make up my mind to seven weeks up here and you doing all the work at home but I finely did it.

All the time I've been here I've wanted to be at home and some times I could hardly stand it but managed to stick it out.

Three weeks ago I engaged a school for six months, two months at $33 and four month at $35, to begin the first Monday in Sept. It is a fine school, the eldest pupil this winter would be a girl of 14 years of age. a good boarding place and the only objection was that it was twenty miles from home.

I thought if I got that suit that I would have that three weeks to catch up the work and could pinch through with out a stitch of sewing for my self. I can send word to Mr. Weaver that I am not going to teach this fall and winter and help you till my time is out and teach next spring I was going to get home before Sunday if possible and suprise you and was going to tell you about my school then

I thought I could repay the money and later give some of the younger ones the chance I always wanted but couldn't have

I would have put it off until next summer but wouldent have the money and couldn't ask for it then It has been *hard* work. I lied when I said I enjoyed it and now when I have spent the time and money that belonged to you I find that you would rather I had done what I wanted to.

It has all been a mistake but it is too late now.

I will come home as soon as possible and make up for lost time.

Out of the 93 who took the exam's 57 failed.

Good bye

Elisabeth Corey

Still only seventeen, Bess obtained her three-month temporary teaching permit—to last until she turned eighteen in November—and began her teaching career in a rural school near a tiny settlement on the railroad line called Tennant (now a ghost town), about five miles west of Harlan and perhaps twenty miles from Corey Farm. There is conflicting information concerning whether Bess taught at Shelby #1, located east of Tennant on land belonging to C. J. Byam, or Shelby #2, south of Tennant in the southeast corner of the F. A. Miller farm. Both schools reportedly looked alike. She may even have taught at both of them, since her letters in March and April 1906 imply that she changed schools.

While teaching in Tennant, she first boarded with the Weaver/ Wever family. A farmer, G. W. Weaver, and his wife, Vashti, along with their children Adelbert and Ida, are listed on the 1900 federal census, and the family also shows up again on the 1905 state census with two more children: Girtie and Lee.

Bess mentions three things that might explain why she moved in with another family before her school term was out. In September, her first letter home describes how small her room is and then says, "I don't know whether there is any chance of my changing my boarding place or not." Then, on January 28, she refers to strained relations between herself and Mrs. Wever, telling her mother "I believe [Mrs. Wever] kind of likes me a little now, that is she dont dislike me the way she did." And in several letters she implies that the Wevers' son Bert, whom she often calls "Brother Wever," may have had a crush on her. Whatever the reason, Bess moved in with another family—the Shaffers—sometime between March 3 and March 28, 1906. According to the 1905 state census, there was a Shaffer family consisting of George Sr., Iowa G., Mabel, George Jr., and Glen (no ages or relationships recorded). There is

This building was identified by Margaret Nelson (daughter of Bess's sister Ethel) as a schoolhouse where Bess once taught. Phil Gerber's note on the envelope containing the photo is "School was moved--now a storage shed." The photo, taken in June 1991, may be of the building listed on the Preservation Iowa website as the one-room school that is located two-and-a-half miles west of the intersection of Highways 59 and 44 in Harlan.

also a Robert and Elizabeth Shaffer household close by, as well as a Shaffer family consisting of W. M., Kate, Robert, Sonia, Hazel R., and Hellen.

SEPTEMBER 10, 1905 TENNANT, IOWA

To Mrs. E. O. Corey

Dear Ma and the rest,—Well this is Sunday and I am going to try and answer up six or eight of the letters I owe.

My School House is a dandy. it is not quite as large as the one at home. It had a new floor put in last spring and the entire inside including ceiling is wainscoated It has been painted inside and out as I had been told that it would be. It faces the west, has three windows on each side, no halls and it has an organ, globe, a number of good maps and all the oldest seats have been replaced with new ones.

The school yard is fenced with a board fence on three sides but open t'ward the road. There is a well and pump in the school yard but the water will not be fit to drink untill it has been pumped dry once or twice

The coal house[1] which has been well filled the past week is two or three rods from the school house door and the school yard has a good many patches of sand burs which with a number of other things are apt to make my school a "howling success."

Every thing has gone pretty well in spite of my receiving the enclosed note and a number of other little trials with which I presume all teachers must contend.

There are seven girls and twelve boys in my school.

I am starting a class of four or five beginers and have a class who wish to finish the eighth grade next spring

I have done some grading and still have twenty eight recitations during the day

The pupils had the "can't habit" pretty bad at first but are getting over it.

Tennant is about two miles from here but on account of no road and the creek not bridged they have to go five or six miles to get there.

I went to Tennant with Mr Wever yesterday morning and went up to Harlan on the nine o'clock train.

I saw the Superintendent and gave him my first weeks report and saw Mrs Parkir[2] and subscribed for some Journels and got some plan books.

I took dinner at Stewarts and was glad to hear that Mrs Stewart is feeling much better. She has not had an operations yet and don't know whether she will or not. Miss Anna Stewart was up a few days ago and since then has been thinking of taking C. S. treatment and was wishing she had the address of some good Healer but I have none with me.

I came down to Corley[3] on the 3:20 train. I went up to Aunt Jennies. They were not at home so I left one of your cards and as I didn't put my name on it I will have to write here soon or she will think that you called on her during her absence When I arrived here a week ago today I was shown up to my room which is a south room with one windo and about the size and shape of that south room up stairs a[t] Copleys. It was furnished with a rag carpet, a bed, a stand, a chair and not a sign of a closet or hook of any sort but when I came home Monday from school there was a row of hook on the wall and a looking glass hanging over the stand.

I don't know whether there is any chance of my changing my boarding place or not.

I will close now hoping to hear from you soon I remain as ever

Elisabeth F. Corey

Tennant, Ia.

P.S. If you cant get Kate to help you threshing time perhaps Emma Nelson would. She is at home now and she could likely come for a few days.

[Enclosure:]

Sep 6th 1905

Miss Corey—

Dear Friend I would like for you to let Ruth go on in her Arithmetic as she is not satisfied atol and dont want to go to school and I may just as well let her stay at home if you are going to keep her back for the rest so hope you will let her go where she left off and Oblige

Mrs[4]

1. A shed that would be filled with coal to feed the schoolhouse stove during the winter months; among Bess's duties was the building of a fire before school began in the morning.

2. A Mrs. Parker is mentioned on page 415 (note 3) in *Bachelor Bess* as being county superintendent of schools in Shelby County (CMW).

3. Corley is where James D. and Jennie Corey Dunlavy, Bess's uncle and aunt, lived at this time (CMW).

4. There is no surname here, nor are there erasure marks (CMW).

SEPTEMBER 17, 1905 TENNANT, IOWA

To Mrs. E. O. Corey

Dear Ma and the rest,—

Well I have finished the second week of school and yesterday it rained quite hard all the forenoon and in the afternoon I washed and went to the great city of Tennant with Miss Ida. Was glad to receive your card and the two papers

I have twenty three pupils enrolled and the school is keeping up its reputation for absent marks as we have had fourty nine in two weeks If the weather down there is any thing like it is up here I don't suppose you have threshed yet. I *hope* you have though.

Wevers threshed before school began

Say this little Lee Wever is as much of a mimic as Paulie and as he thinks "The School Maam" is about alright and a pretty nice "kid" he mimics every thing I do or say.

I have gained ten pounds since I came up here and weigh two hundred and ten pounds. how is that for size?

My pupils sized me up pretty well the first morning and all I have to do is to start after them and they howl as if their time had come.

I have some mischievous little scamps and I like them better, if anything than the good ones.

There is one boy about nine years of age and he looks enough like Rob Corey at that age to have been his twin. The other day he got into mischief just before school let out so I called him up to the recitation seat to study I then opend a book and placing my elboes on my desk pretended to read but in reality I was watching him between my fingers. Of cource as soon as I put my head down he screwed up his face (just like Rob) and ran his tongue out two or three inches. I straightend up and looked at him and the expression on his face said as plain as words "I'm in for it." I told him to turn around and make that face for the school to see He wouldn't so I gave him a good shaking. You've seen children play roten egg? Well he looked like one that had been shook hard and then broke. The idea struck me so forceably and so funny that I turned on my heel and went to my desk saying sternly take your seat. Oh! how he howled and no wonder for he knew his brother would tell at home and his father would give him a good thrashing. But the strange part of it is that he never attempted to fight me and he has fought every teacher he ever went to school to before

It must be because I was such a bad egg when I went to school but it seems as though I could tell what each one is going to do and how they are going to take things nine times out of ten.

I rode to school with the cream man on muddy morning

I've done a good deal of sewing and mending but have a good deal to do yet.

I believe I have a good Director one that will stand by me through thick and thin if I do the square thing

There are so many funny things happen in school, that if I had a good book for it, I would keep a Journal.

One boy came to school with his pants on wrong side out. Another little fellow found a sand bur in school time and exclamed "Get out of this you old sand bur."

Will close hoping to hear from you soon

I remain

Elisabeth F. Corey.

[written in top margin of first page:] It has rained most every day for two weeks. We have no R.F.D. and it is so hard to send or get mail

. . . .

SEPTEMBER 23, 1905 TENNANT, IOWA

To Mrs. E. O. Corey

Dear mamma,—I am going to write you another letter and, if the third time is the lucky one, perhaps you will get it.

If someone would put something under that Marne Post Office and blow it up they might find the fragments of a number of lost letters. If you haven't received my other two letters by this time you better say something to *Cousin Charlie* about it.

My third week of school has been much like the other two with the exception of a discovery that I made. I discovered that there are two familys who just about live on lies and the children are as bad as their folks & were telling some about me, as I had given no one reason for telling such things I was perfectly thunder struck, in fact, I was almost to surprised to be angry for a minute and I almost tremble to think what might have happened if I had not been so suprised.

I guess most everyone takes there lies for what they are worth so it isn't so bad but you can imagine how I felt for a little while.

I've got a colt to break in next week. I am curious to know how much kicking will be done

Tell Fuller I heard Gertie Wever telling at school that she had seen one of teachers brothers so she had Four of Mrs Pete Nelson's brother's children go to school to me and are just a[s] nice as they can be.

I hope your threshings done and your Harlan trip over. How many times did you get ready for threshers?

This pencil is in bad need of sharpening and Bert has gone to bed so I can't go after a knife so will close and remain

Elisabeth Corey,

c/o G. W. Wever. Tennant, Ia

. . . .

OCTOBER 5, 1905 TENNANT, IOWA

To Mrs. E. O. Corey, Elmdale

Dear ma,—I wrote you a letter several days ago but as it didn't get mailed I guess I will write you another one.

Did you and Rob get rained on before you got home?

How does Paul like his pantz? One day we were talking about nick-names and I said that we all had nicknames. Gertie ask right of[f] what we called the one that brought me up here. I told her that was "Toad" and when she heard me ask you if some of the Boys were com-ming up she said "Oh maybe Toad will come!"

Miss Ida Cutshell's sisterinlaw, Mrs Harvey Cutshell taught this school for two years before she was married. She was out here visiting Wevers Tues. and Wednesday.

Mrs Sam Buckley, Martha Wever that used to be, came out last Tuesday and has been here ever since. Frank is staying here and going to school and I guess she came out for a while to keep him from get-ting homesick.

There has been from two to six extras here for the last week.

Oh! how I want to see some of you folks!

Please write as often as you can or have some of the rest write.

You know that gray skirt? well its so tight across the hips that I cant wear it. I can't think of any way of changing it either.

Well I must close and go to bed so good bye
Yours As Ever
Elisabeth F. Corey
Tennant, Ia

. . . .

OCTOBER 12, 1905 TENNANT, IOWA

To Mrs. E. O. Corey, Elmdale
Dear mamma,—

Well how are you anyway? How's the cave?[1] How did the boys get home? When will the boys start corn husking? Did Rob ask Mary [Lanigan] if she got my letter? What's the matter with Harrises? Has Olney sent for that quarterly?

I haven't my order cashed yet and don't know when I will get it cashed.

Wevers buchered the other day after it turned cold and we have had fresh meat and lots of it every meal since

This evening when I got about half way home I met Mrs Wever comming over after me. She said that Gertie thought I was sick.

The folks here all got out their knitting the other evening and so I got out that head shall [shawl] and am making quite a showing on it. Bert makes all kinds of fun of my *"cedar posts"* as he calls them. He says he is going to bring up a couple of cedar posts some evening and start him a shall. He was examining my shall the other evening and I asked him what he would give me to make him one and he said "A deal of a lot of yarn and a couple of cedar posts"

I have half a notion to knit me some mittens. Those old gloves got so wholey that I left them over to the school house to build fires with and my fingers most freeze these cold mornings.

Its lots of fun knitting when Mrs Wever and the girls are at it too and Bert reads to us and sings a song once in a while to keep us awake.

I don't know what I would do if it wasn't for remembering that I'll be home in less than three weeks, occasionly.

Those socks wont do me much good as I forgot my patern.

Guess I will close for now and remain as ever
Elisabeth F. Corey
Tennant, Ia

c/o G. W. Wever

PS

Saturday Oct 14 1905

My! how it has rained since I got home last night and it looks like it might keep it up all day.

I don't believe Wevers will go to town today and I haven't had my mail for a week. Yesterday Ruth said that Elmer said he saw a letter addressed to me in Wevers box so of course I am anxious to get the mail

Two young gentlemen visited our school yesterday one of them is from California and has been visiting relatives in these parts

Yours as Ever E. F. C.

1. The cave refers to a springhouse carved into a slope, probably along Indian Creek, which ran through Corey Farm. Milk and other dairy products could be kept fresh in its cool interior.

• •

NOVEMBER 29, 1905 TENNANT, IOWA

To Mrs. E. O. Corey

Dear mamma and the rest,—

Well I have not heard from any of you as yet but suppose I will the next time any one goes to Tennant

Oh we just had the greatest time here!! I told Gertie to ask the director if he was going to give us Thanksgiving day and she said the next day that he said if I wanted it he would have to as it was against the law to *make* a teacher teach on Thanksgiving Day. Well I never thought anything more about it till Wednesday the 22nd when Mrs Miller was talking about the 23 being Thanks giving Day and I said no it was the 30th. Then we got to disputing and they finely owned that I was right and Mrs Miller said Why she had sent Wevers their Thanks giving goose already. Well at school I discovered that part of the people were going to celebrate the 23 and some the 30th. Gertie said it was the 23rd that the director gave us so after school I went over to Wevers. I didn't see the director but I saw the directoress and got things straightened out so I taught last Thursday and will not have to teach tomorrow. Well we got up this morning to find things froze up solid and a dust of snow. it is snowing again now quite hard.

It rained Monday and there was travel enough yesterday to make it about as rough as roads could be

Is the cave finished? are the boys through husking? have the boys started in school? how is everything?

Mr Miller and Willie are going to Avoca and will mail this. We all picked geese for market last night—was up till most eleven.

I attended the Sunday School Convention in Tennant Saturday—had a talk with Anna Stewart and an introduction to more people than I can begin to remember the names of.

Am going to Corley Friday evening and to Harlan Sat. and up to Anna Stewarts a week from Saturday.

I guess I cant make a connection to take music lessons this winter

I didn't have to walk to Tennant a week ago Tues. evening either—Emma[,] Walter and I went—just had lots of fun.

Have you driven Rat to the topbuggy yet? does he think it as bad as an umbrella Well it is about school time so must close for now Guess you better return that yarn and things for if I need it I can get it up here

Good by write often

Bess.

P.S. Please send me an account of what I owe you on those vacation purchases and tell Toad to send me an account of the expense he is going to on account of the shelter for the buggy. E. F. C.

If I furnish the envelopes some of you folks ought to write often

[Written upside-down on first page:] Next time you write please put in a pair of sock tops for my underware ends.

[At the top of page 2, written sideways:] I have seventeen pupils now. Its blizzarding some now and fearful cold

· ·

DECEMBER 4, 1905 TENNANT, IOWA

To Mrs. E. O. Corey, Elmdale

Dear folks,—Well we had our roast goose Thursday and I finished that skirt that I was faceing up with the blue serge one—it is nice and warm these days.

Friday evening after school I walked over to Corley—about five miles it was awful rough and it was quite dark when I got there I got my mail just before I started—three letters and your card—didn't read them till I got over to Aunt Jen's—I was sorry to hear about Mr Copleys death. I must write to them.

I got a letter from Alma Johansen. I didn't know till I got to Dunlavys that there wasn't any morning train to Harlan but as Aunt Jen was going up across the country I went along—We went in the fore noon and didnt leave Harlan till sun down in the evening.

I went to the dentist and he said I had three wisdom teeth through alright and the one I had been having trouble with was two thirds through but my jaw was full of teeth with out it and it was coming in farther back so I had to have it pulled he got his hatchets and things ground up then went to work he cut out a piece of my gum about the size of your foot then after cutting the rest of the gum free from the tooth he put that what you call it of his in my mouth and took a hold of that tooth as if it was a bad boy, he wiggled it and twisted it and pulled it untill he got tired of fooling and then he yanked it out. you aught to have heard the exclamation he made when it came out, he said it was an "*awful big tooth*" he filled one for me while he was at it.

I went to the photographers, the book store, the jewelers, and to a drygoods store; I got me some knitting needles in a wooden case so you can return those others if you dont want them yourself. I went up to Stewarts just a few minutes I just missed Mrs Stewart as she had just gone down town. I promised Sarah I would come up and stay over Saturday with her some time soon. Andrew has his new house nearly completed and will be married soon. *By Jing*

I saw Mrs Smith and talked to her a little while. She left Lida at home. Lida is teaching the Bacon school two miles north of mine.

We are going to walk over to Tennant to revival tomorrow evening I guess.

Did the boys get the corn out before the snow? Has Toadie started in school yet? I suppose Olney starts in this morning.

'Tis school time will close for now.

December 5

Well I'll try to finish my letter Mr. Miller went to Avoca today and I could have had it mailed if it had been finished

Sunday forenoon Aunt Jen had me trim the tail of that black skirt of hers. Uncle Jim was just full of the Old Nick and teased Aunt Jen till he almost drove her crazy finely I gave her a pin to stick him with then he began to plague me—He said he wouldn't mind being fat but he *would hate* to be *all* fat. I told him I didn't mind being tall but *gosh* I *would hate* to be *all* tall. Uncle Jim doubled up like a jackknife for a minute then he went down to the Post Office.

Say if Uncle Jim is ever at our house again when I am there, you just keep out of the kitchen and turn the cooking over to me and if I don't make his old stomach ache it's because he has a steel one with brass screws or has turned Christian Scientist or something else extraordinary.

I showed Aunt Jen how she could trim her own skirts and not have to wait for some one else to do it for her and she said, "Why I never thought of *that* before!"

I guess we wont go to Tennant this evening after all.

I got started on my brown skirt last evening.

Must close so some of you write soon

E. F. Corey

[Written at the top and in the margin of page 1:] December 6 I will put this in my Last envelope so can not enclose one. Gertie is going to mail this and get my mail this evening. I have finished putting that flounce on my brown skirt and am wearing it today That makes the fourth big job of sewing Ive done—will start to line my coat tonight I think.

. . . .

DECEMBER 9, 1905 TENNANT, IOWA

To Mrs. E. O. Corey, Elmdale

Marne, Iowa

Dear folks,—I finely got Gertie to mail that last letter to you and as she put it in a mail box I don't know when you will get it. I thought I would write you a little more as some of Millers are going to Avoca and I can get it mailed.

The "Protracted Meeting"[1] over to Tennant is getting a lot of "convicts" as Frank Fish said. They have got one hundred scalps already. Several of my pupils have gone forward but what does it amount to any way?

I went last evening. Emma, Walter, and I planed to walk over but the three McKeighan children came over with the spring wagon and took us.

Nellie was just full of the old Nick going over so I was kind of glad when she got religeon and went forward cause I thought perhaps she would behave her self going home but no she acted worse than ever and Walter who is ever so much like Fuller could hardly stand it. at last he said "Say what was you thinkin' about when you was settin' on your knees up there?" Nellie didn't answer him so pretty soon he said "Say I thought you was cryin'" and Nellie said "Why yes they all do" and there she had done the whole thing just because the rest did and I doubt if she has ever spent ten minutes of serious thought on the subject. Such religeon! Ba-a-a

The lady preacher came around and asked me if I was a Christian what a questian! How is a person to know any way? I told her I tried to be one and she asked me if I succeeded and I dont know what I said I guess I stammered out something to the effect that I didn't know.

Coming home Emma said "Why teacher she called you sister an I didn't know she was any relation of yours.["] I said, "Didn't you?" She said "No but she seemed to have lots of relatives there." Emma will never hear the last of that

I dont know whether to go out to Stewarts this afternoon or not

Must close in haste so write soon

As Ever

Bess

1. A revival meeting (PG). The *Shelby County Republican* (December 28, 1905) described the three-week event as "rather remarkable," having effected eighty conversions. The three-page article also mentions two other revivals in Iowa that are waging "systematic war on sin" across the state (CMW).

· ·

DECEMBER 10, 1905 TENNANT, IOWA

To J. Olney Corey, Walnut, Iowa

Dear Brother,—Hello, how's the weather down there? Mighty warm up here now, while the revivals last.

I heard once that they had gotten one hundred scalps but found out later that it was only twenty seven new members and twenty three of them "convicts" as Frank said.

Tuesday evening three of the children and I went over to the school house for some books, we were well armed I asure you, I carried a lantern, Emma her "billy club," Walter the shot gun and I don't remember what Eddie had.

Walter, Emma and I planed to walk to Tennant Friday evening but McKeighans came over and took us. I saw quite a few that I knew.

Yesterday I did my washing and blistered my knuckles on the washboard and then got ready and went over to Tennant, I 'phoned over to Anna Stewart and she and Will met me there after church and took me out to their home. Anna and I soon retired but talked till most two before we went to sleep.

We attended Sunday School and church at Pioneer today and Anna and Ellen brought me over to Millers this evening.

I received a letter from home Saturday (yesterday) evening, Ma and Ethel both wrote.

Four of the little pupils I had last fall are not going this winter but I have twenty enrolled and the two Miller boys will start tomorrow I almost forgot to tell you that I had the great pleasure of meeting Mr. Henry Cook one of Mr. Harlan Cook's brothers, they are both "just lovely" as the girls say

I've been making Xmas cards just to see what I could do, they are white card board with gilt edges and a picture some thing like this in the center

and a spray of holly at the top and the pupils name at the bottom.

Guess I will enclose you some cards for if you have got to be such a "swell" young gent you may need some. Who are your teachers?[1] How do you like it? How are you getting along? Can you 'phone to mamma with out paying? How's pa and ma Copley?

I must close now and go over the lesson so write soon.

Love to all

Bess.

1. Olney Corey had entered the public school at Walnut and was boarding, as Bess had, with the Copley family.

Letterhead Bess used to write several of her letters.

DECEMBER 17, 1905 TENNANT, IOWA

To Mrs. E. O. Corey, Elmdale

Hello folks how do you like my new paper? We're going to have the Mail Route[1] next spring they say and they have the new road opened up so that its passable.

I got your last letter a week ago Saturday—I went out to Stewarts that evening and came back Sunday evening—had a fine time—attended church and Sunday School at Pioneer with the Stewarts.

I have as big a school now as I had last fall and there is more to start yet.

I received a very interesting note from a much interested mamma not long ago. I do so like to see parents *interested* in the school!! My school is to give an intertainment the first Thursday in January. I think it will be a good one.

I have finished my first month of school this term and yesterday when Millers went to Avoca I rode down as far as Bohlanders and got my order and as I am going to Tennant tomorrow I may send you a P.O. money order for twenty.

Mrs Bohlander used to be Miss Rosa Wunder who taught in Marne when Irma Copley taught there—she met papa in Avoca several years ago with her brother Fred of whom I've heard papa speak.

One day I heard Willie speak about going to school to Miss Halway in Avoca. I ask him which one and he said it was Anna, Laura's younger sister.

One day Gertie was talking about when she lived in Hastings Nebraska and I ask her if she ever heard of the name of Edgeton and she said yes the Edgeaton boys were her cousins and that Goldie Edgeaton was a second cousin of hers—you know Goldie is a cousin of the Copley young folks and that was where Mrs Copley was visiting last fall.

This evening Mrs Miller was telling about some people she used to know in Denmark who came to this country after they did and lived near Lewis for some years and then moved up north—their name was Christensen—Sorn Christensens, and I was just wondering if those were the people living near Rorbeck.

"It do beat all" how I run acrossed folks dont it.

Mr and Mrs Wever were here a little while this afternoon they had been over to the school house splitting up wood for me. Mr Wever said he saw my Uncle John at a sale near Corley the other day and he didn't believe that till then that Uncle John knew I was teaching up here—I said don't you believe it my uncle isn't so ignorant of my whereabouts as he might be

Its queer he could be visiting Dunlevy's and never find out that I was in this part of the country.

I guess the meeting in Tennant hasn't got as many converts as I once heard although they have quite a number—Ida Wever went forward a week ago and was baptised this morning.

I received a letter from Lida Smith the other day, it was a real long one and she is as much of a tearer as ever.

Oh!! such times as I have here at Millers!!! The boys have got to locking me in my room every chance they get and I have to make a deal of a racket befor any one hears me and lets me out. of course its one of the seven boys but who knows which?

I don't know about Xmas it makes me most sick to think about it.

Walter is such a tease tonight he said "You can ride our old mule if you want to—she's got the heaves awfully bad but he's tough and will keep right on a walkin' and if you start from here at five o'clock you can get there by noon and stay alnight and come home the next day."

I expect to get those buttons or pins rather next time I go to town and will send them to you as soon as I get them. The two largest pins with papa's picture on are for you and you can give one of them to grandma for a Xmas present—it will likely be as acceptable as any thing from you could be and I think she would like it.

Its alright about your not writing I know you are "awful" busy but

I thought the children might write some times—that was a nice letter Ethel wrote me.

My! its such a relief to know you have the corn out and the things down cellar

Well I must close as Emma is waiting to help me make Xmas cards. I guess I'll enclose some little ones for Ethel to give her school mates.

Good By. Yours as Ever

Bess.

P.S. Being so busy is a tax on a fellow—I have more than thirty recitations and its worse than scrubbing floors or paper hanging—I get up at half after seven and get to school by eight,—I've quit eating breakfast entirely for it was just a wast of time as I have to eat dinner any way,—I dig all day till five o'clock, then come home and wash and comb and eat supper and then am at some thing or other hard till between half after eleven and half after twelve.

I'm afraid I'll get sour if I keep it up so I guess I'll take Valerie's advise and get a fellow to take me around some—there's one consolation I wont have to take one that she has bounced any way.

I don't find money so plenty these days even if you can get a dollar for for [*sic*] fifty five and forty five cents.

Bess—

1. The R.F.D. (Rural Free Delivery) system was spreading rapidly throughout rural America.

. . . .

DECEMBER 18, 1905 TENNANT, IOWA

To Mrs. E. O. Corey

Dear Ma,—I wrote you last evening with the intention of going to Tennant this evening but as Willie went this morning after I went to school we got the mail and we gave up going this evening and as your letter did not get mailed I will write you another one

It's alright about the boys not writing I know they must be pushed all the time so I'll try to be satisfied if I hear from you once in a while—just soak your feet next time you write to me, it will [be] all right if you dont get the writing to me done althoug I'm glad to hear from you any time I expect if you folks had known what Uncle John told Mr Wever you would have booted him off the place—it's darned mean of 'em to act so.

Oh! Why did you speak of Christmas? You can surely stand it if I can. No I don't see any hope of my getting home—it would cost me more by train by the time I got back than If I hired a team to take me clear through or as much and I guess I'm too stingy for that this year. You needn't worry about my being out after dark for I have some sence if I haven't the dollars and I can protect my self and I don't make a buisness of being alone after dark either.

I received a note from Mrs. Dunlavey this evening she didn't invite me to spend Xmas with her either.—When you see John Corey tell him that if he didn't lie some one else did.

Good by and a Merry Christmas and Happy New Year to all of you.
Bess

P.S. How often does Olney get home Tell Ethel I'll try and get that song for her. E. F. C.

· ·

DECEMBER 29, 1905 TENNANT, IOWA

To Mrs. E. O. Corey

Dear folks,—How did Olney get home? I was sorry that he couldn't stop here alnight but they were so crowded—suppose he had a fine time at our "*Uncles*." I hope so any way.

I retired very early Monday evening and got up Tuesday morning with a worse cold than ever—its some better now—I can actually get a whole sentence said out loud.

Our entertainment is coming on fine and will be in proper shape by Jan 4th I guess—the girls are so interested in some of the boys coming up they speak oftenest of Fuller as they feel best acquainted with him—Gertie says "Why they could stay all night at our house so as not to have to go back the same day."—and when I told Gertie about Olneys debate[1] she said "That's good." "Oh tell him when you see him I'm awful glad he won."

Better not tell Toad that till after Olney goes back to school if you want to keep peace in the family.

Ruth Myers laid her report card on my desk the other morning without a word and I noticed that it was her mothers signature in the proper place—I consider every victory won without blood shed a feather in my cap

Wevers shelled last Tuesday and just before school was out *Brother Wever* brought a load of cobs over and put them in the cob house in fine shape he said they were good and husky and would burn easy— I've heard a little more about *Brother* Wever getting married—just heard the girls name that was all—there may be some thing in it but I would sooner think it was one of Gertie's lies. bet he would swear if he knew she told *that.*

I suppose you have heard long before this of Mrs Stewart's death and burial. I didn't hear of her death till after her burial Tuesday— what a sad Christmas for Sarah—poor girl—Say I was just wondering if she wouldn't go and keep house for that brother of hers who lost his wife last fall

I wrote Sarah a note Tuesday evening but didn't get it mailed till just today

I haven't been doing much these evenings—havent done a thing to my waist but my cold has seemed so bad that sometimes I couldn't say more than three words out loud in that many sentences in fact I almost lost my voice entirely and of course that was excuse enough for some of them to act as mean as sin so by the time I got home at night I was ready to go to bed. If it hadn't of held off till I got back up here I wouldn't be up here yet.

I'm going to Harlan in the morning so must close for now with love to all

Bess.

1. Competitive oratorical and debate contests were common on the high-school level during this period.

· ·

DECEMBER 31, 1905 TENNANT, IOWA

To Mrs. E. O. Corey, Elmdale

Dear Folks,—Well if I'm going to write you another letter this year I'll have to hurry.

Yesterday I arose bright and early, but not quite early enough, and dressed in my Sunday go to Preachin clothes and started out for Tennant—I went the new road as it was much the shortest—and roughest too I found The train, for a wonder, was just on time and my watch was just a little behind time and of course the darned old train wouldn't wait for me so I waited for the next one.

Well the next passenger train dont go till 6:20 in the evening but there was a Way Freight due there at 10:10 and *What men have done women may do*, and as Mat said lots of times the Tennant ladies did, I decided to go up on that so I purchased my ticket and got my permit then proceeded to wait and I just keept on proceeding till half after one then continued my journey with the baggage man, brakman, and a jug for traveling companions

Reached Harlan alright and went up to see the Co. Supt.—had quite a talk with him—I ask him what to do about the parents not getting nescessary books for the children and he said if I couldn't persuade the parents to get the books I better get along with out them and use lots of outside work then I ask him when he thought I could get in the *outside work* and hear thirty three recitations a day—of course that was *different*—he went and got my report and looked it over and said he was coming down to visit my school—I told him about our entertainment and he said for me to anounce to the children that he would be at their entertainment and talk to them a while after their program—and said he might visit my school before that time so I'm in for a week of it.

I went up to Stewarts—found Lida Smith there and after we had talked a while we agreed to stay alnight so we went down town to get our shopping done—we had lots of fun and with lots to do we didn't get back to Stewarts till about six o'clock

While we were down town we went up to the central office and I was going talk to you as it would not cost me any thing—after we got connection I found that my cold was still so bad you couldn't understand me so Lida had to do the talking—she said she could hear every word you said and I was standing several feet away but could hear part of what you said but Lida said you couldn't hear any thing she said for she could hear some one tell you every word. I mailed you a letter but knew you wouldnt get it till this week some time and thought I would call you up so you wouldnt worry.

Sarah is very thin and rather pale but I failed to see the gray hairs Alice told about but then of course I didn't take her down and hunt for them.

I had quite a visit with Sarah but of course not quite as good a one as I would have had if Lida hadn't been there but when Sarah was busy she entertained me in the kitchen and Lida entertained George in the sitting room

Sarah said that three weeks ago after I had been there she just wished she had *insisted* on my staying all night and when her mother came home from down town she seemed to feel so bad about missing connections with me and that made Sarah think of it that much more and it was just the next Tuesday that her mother was taken sick and was never conscious for more than a minute or two at a time after that and she died about nine o'clock a week ago Saturday morning and was buried last Tues.

Sarah spoke as if she was going on keeping house for George there in town but she is awful lonesome and when I spoke about going to get me some longesleved aprons she said to get the stuff and come up some Friday after school and she would cut them out for me Friday evening and I could make them Saturday—Now wasn't that good of her?

Lida and I looked great in Sarah's night clothes and we all three slept in one bed. We all started out for church this morning—to the Congregational—I guess that's what they call it,—but instead of a serman we heard a fine talk on the "Boy Problem" by Mr. Ed Denison of Atlantic whom I met some four or five years ago. I had a little talk with him afterward, he is a Y.M.C.A. worker and his talk was realy the best thing I've heard for a long time

We went home from church and had dinner—after we got the dishes done we discovered that it was nearly train time but as Dick was harnessed and the train was usually late George wasn't in much of a hurry but finely went over to a neighbors and phoned down to the depot and they said the train was on time he pulled out his watch and found that it was a minute passed time he came back on the run, and he is quite a picture on the run, and began to hitch up so I got my wraps on and when he drove around I took his coat out to him and pretty soon we was going some for the station—we got there and I went in and asked when the train would be there and they said in about five minutes so I went out and talked to George till he got froze out—he promised to bring Sarah down some time.

I wasted a penny to get weighed and just weighed 206½ with my wraps on and I was dress awful heavy beside—I guess its all hokus pokus about my getting thin but I realy am growing a trifle in highth—am about 5 ft 7 in now—that up with the tallest Corey women.

I saw a young lady get on the train ahead of me and when I started to pass her seat she raised up and ask if I wasn't "Miss Corey." I said that I was and she introduced herself as Matilda Trottner (Henry's sister)—she said Sarah Schuster said she thought I was Miss Corey. So I had some one to talk to all the way down—when we got to Tennant her folk were so crowded I couldn't ride out with them and as it was about church time I went to church—Rev Mr Stephenson delivered the sermon—he is the Bishop or Elder or what ever you call it.

his sermon was just fine—next to C. S.

I saw most every body I knew and I spoke to that horrid Bert Wever twice and he never heard me—bet if I ever speak to him again he'll hear alright.

I rode out two miles with Elizabeth Best and walked the rest of the way—got home about dark.

I received a postal from Aunt Jen, the other day in answer to my letter guess I will answer it with a card—I'm bound she shant say that I broke the correspondance.

Now instead of answering this letter you better write me a card and soak your feet in the coffee while your at it and then go to bed and we will both live *jest* as long and the world wont go round any faster. I must close for now—with love

Bess

· ·

JANUARY 7, 1906 TENNANT, IOWA

To Mrs. E. O. Corey

Dear folks,—Well if I remember aright I haven't written you since some time last year and many interesting things have hapened since then

Of course we had a great time getting ready for our entertainment—But to begin with the first of the year—Last Monday when I entered the school house I was suprised to find that it had been thoroughly cleaned so we started in the new year with a clean house

About noon Monday Gertie asked me if I had found any thing in my desk—I thought she was guying[1] so I said yes but pretty soon she said something else and I got suspicious and opened my desk to discover some candy in tisue paper—I pulled it out and looked again and found a stunning handkerchief then I looked the third time and found a little note which was signed in cipher but as I recognized the writing I easily made out the signature. [written at top of page, upside down: I had been to my desk three or four times that morning and never saw those things.]

All the fore part of the week we were busy getting ready—we used bed blankets for curtains and as we could not afford curtain rings we sewed twine string on this way [a small drawing here looks like a snake wiggling on a line] and strung twine through to run them on it was lots of bother but it worked allright

We gave our entertainment Thurs. evening to a full house and it was pronounced "fine"

Henry and Matilda Trottner helped me clear through just fine—Matilda read the programe for me which left me free to superintend the dressing rooms which was quite necessary.

The Superintendant and Vincent Robinsen were there and Mr Luxford made a speech and I'll tell you a bad one on him alrighty—In the cource of his speech he told that little storey about the dogs tail and after wards the children said he told the same storey at Center School house and at the school picnic and they thought he better get another one pretty soon

My how cold it is! I wrote that last or rather first part of my letter in bed to keep warm but froze out even there that is my fingers got so cold I couldn't write and beside that my pencil was such a poor one I couldn't make much headway.

I got my new waist done in time to wear to our entertainment but I had to work pretty late two evenings to do it—One evening I was sewing and Mrs Miller was knitting and Walter was setting around teasing and wouldnt go to bed, about ten oclock Mr Miller went out and discovered that the ground was white with snow so about twelve when I was putting away my sewing Walter dared me to comeout and snow ball so we wrapped up and went out for a snow battle—Mrs Miller came out to act as judge and she decided in my favor as I only failed to hit him twice.—we got in about half past twelve

Last evening we went over to Wevers—Walter Emma and I we just had a fine time—McKeighans were there too—we played games and ate popcorn and cake—we played cross questions and crooked answers and I never saw answers fit so well—one boys question was "Will you marry me" and my answer to it was "I guess so."

I will put some of the other questions and answers on the next page

"When did you see Henry last?" "Yesterday at half past nine."

"Will you be my best girl?" "I'll tell you tomorrow evening at half past eight"

"Who called on you last?" "Sure Mike"

"May I see you at home?" "Why of course."

"May I see you home?" "I'll think about it"

"Did you see John" "No."

"Who was it?" "Miss Corey"

Did you ever see answers fit better than those? I never did.

Mrs Miller hasn't been very well and Walter has turned cook and he makes a pretty good one too.

I know what was the matter with brother Wever. He was mad cause I wouldn't have a box social[2] and now he is ashamed of him self and tries to make out it was someone else I spoke to by mistake—He was awful goody goody last night and talked to me more than all the rest put together.

Ida was teasing him about being so blue all the week and he turned to me and said "Honest a fellow can set around here till he gets so lonesome he almost hates him self"—Gertie heard him and said he aught to go and see his girl and he said he had been to see them all and none of them would let him come again then she said there was one he hadn't gone to see and she thought she would like to have him come too. he asked her who it was and *Jiminie* but I was skeered but she didn't tel him.

I must close for now and answer Alma Johannsen's letter so good by yours as ever

Bess.

1. Joking.

2. A box social was a party to which the ladies anonymously brought decorated boxes of suppers or refreshments and the men bid for the chance to share the food (and perhaps the evening) in the lady's company.

To Mrs. E. O. Corey, Elmdale

Dear folks,—Dont know whether you have received my last letter or not—it was written the *7th*—if you haven't you will so I'll just begin where I left off and tell you the rest up to date.

To begin with—read this over to your self before you read any of it out.

In my last letter you know I spoke of Mrs Miller being sick—well she was feeling pretty bad last Sunday evening and I went in and asked her if there was any-thing I could do—she said no unless I could put up my dinner for the next day so I did.

She told me what was the matter she said it was her time for feeling bad she had run over time and was having it hard—she seemed to have such a headache—

Monday morning I was rather late and didnt go in to see her but asked Mr Miller how she was he said she was better that her head didn't ache but she still had those fainting spells having fainted dead away seven times in the night—well after dinner she made up her mind she wanted to see Mrs Wever so sent over for her and Mrs Wever made them send for the Dr. and when the doctor arived he said if she was a Catholic to send for a priest right away that any breath might be her last there was not a table spoon full of blood left in her body but she got better for a while but Mrs Wever and Mrs Myers sat up alnight

Ida took her pa to the train and her brother was away shelling so she had to leave Lee at the school house.

Monday evening when I got home after school they told me I better go over to Wevers but I said if I could be of any help I would rather stay they said alright so I stayed—I helped Emma with the work and as they were out of bread I started some and worked it down before I went to school Tuesday morning so Emma just had to put it in the pans and bake it.

Tuesday evening when I got home Mrs Wever and Mrs Myers had gone and they were alone and Mrs Miller seemed a little worse the fever was raising and the only way we could keep it down was to keep wet cloths on her head. Mr Miller got skeered and sent Willie down the other side of Avoca for his sister Mrs. Sorensen and then he and

I sat up and took turns putting cloths on her head at the rate of two a minute—she got better twords morning and I went up and had a good sleep before morning then Wednesday she seemed to get worse they sent for Mrs Wever she went over and stayed till last night Willie didn't get home till about nine o'clock Wednesday morning—he had had a dreadfull time—Mrs Sorensen had her leg broke some time back and of course she couldn't come then he had to go farther on to his uncles and finely suceeded in getting his cousin to come—she is about my age—good to work but no good around sick folks—told Mrs Miller the first thing that she was almost dead and Mrs Miller got worse so Wednesday evening Ida came over to the school house after me she said I better go home with her as Mrs Miller wasnt expected to live till morning and as that cousin was there to help with the work and as I could do no good I went and have been staying here ever since

Mrs Miller was a little better Thursday morning and I went down after Ollie and took him to school with me which made it much quieter and every one is so *very* much obliged to me but they needn't be for its a great consolation to have him where I dare spank him when he needs it—I didn't have to though for he was exceptionly good. He was at school all day yesterday

Well thank Heaven Mrs Miller is better and doing nicely but I will likely stay here another week

Brother Wever has just sharpened that pocket knife Rob lent me its just fine and he says it will hold the edge till I get through cutting shaven[1] next time.

Mrs Wever has gone to Shelby after Mr Wever and Ida is sewing and tell Toadie Gertie is baking cake so she can take Walter a piece and Lee has been keeping still for about ten seconds and *Brother Wever* is "Sittin round bein' good" and I'm writing to my ma—whats you all doing Havent had my mail for a long time—Say write me a card some time so I'll know you are alright Ida wants to add a P.S. so I will close and remain as ever with love

Bess.

[In a different handwriting, probably that of Ida Wever:]

A Case of Mistaken Identity.

A young lady coming home from school one evening met a young man and and older man. She knew the young man and thought the old man was the young man's father and spoke to him of course he spoke also and after she had gone on her way he asked the young man if that was his mother. He told him it was the school ma'am. She didn't know the difference until she was told but she gave herself away.

[Back in handwriting of Elizabeth Corey:]

Superintendant Luxford visited school Friday.

Maggie Sorensen is now at Millers I met her years ago up north.

1. Cutting shaven may refer to slicing shavings off a piece of wood as kindling to start a fire in the schoolhouse stove in the morning.

. . . .

JANUARY 21, 1906 TENNANT, IOWA

To Mrs. E. O. Corey

Dear folks,—Hello! Hows the weather down there? Pretty cool up here.

Well as usual I will begin where I left off in my last letter.

I wrote my last letter a week ago yesterday (Saturday the 13) well that after noon I brought out a set of jackstones,[1] the first they had ever seen and that evening Gertie, Brother Wever, and I sat down on the floor and had just a dandy game.

Sunday we had another game or two and I read a good deal— Mrs Wever went over to Millers just before dinner and when she came back she said Mrs Miller was better and she brought me your card a letter from Mary and an advertisment That evening about nine o'clock Walter came after Mrs Wever for his mother was much worse—We retired about as soon as she had gone and arose the next morning to find the ground white with snow and it was still snowing

We had rather a small school that day and that evening Brother Wever came after us in the sled—we stoped at Millers and Mrs W— came out crying and said they had done all they could do that Mrs Miller had given up hope and told him where to bury her and to try to keep the children together and the doctor gave them no encouragement and it was only a matter of time.

We then started out for home but when we were going up that hill north of the school house we got into a drift—one runner cut down and the other didn't just then a gust of wind came along over we went and "rolled in the beautiful—Oh so cold!" The dickens of it is the Hanon and McKeighan boys were still in sight so we never expect to hear the last of it—We thought none of us were hurt but after we got home and warmed up Brother Wever found that he had a bad bruse where he threw himself against the sleigh to keep it from going over onto us

Perhaps you think it sounds sentimental to sit at one side of the table and read while some one sits at the other side of the table and whistles "Sweet Bunch of Daises" or "The Sweetheart That Went Down on The Main" or some such tune and occasionly heaves a sigh.

Tuesday night Mrs Miller was reported the same—Mrs Wever came home in the afternoon they didn't think she would last till morning but Wednesday the Dr said she was a little better

Walter came for Mrs Wever again Wednesday morning and she came home Thursday afternoon and said Mrs Miller was still improving

The nurse and Mrs Wever had a rumpus with some of Millers Dane relations—they came up there and wouldnt help any and just raised Ned—they were bound to go in and talk to Mrs Miller after the Dr. said that no one should be alowed in the room

Friday the doctor said Mrs Miller was getting along alright if that other desease didnt start in I've forgotten what the name of it is but any way the glands of the body swell up and the blood changes to water and yesterday they said it had started and no power on earth could save her—Mrs Wever is over there now to find out how she is so I will be able to tell you the latest before I close my letter to you

Yesterday Mr Bailey and his son were here to dinner but they had teased me so much about my mistaking him for Mr W__ that I wouldn't go out to dinner

I heard Brother Wever ask "Where's the Schoolma'am" and Ida said "she asked to be excused" then he asked what was the matter and, Mrs Wever said "bashfulness I guess" but Brother Wever knew what was the trouble and after dinner he came in and asked me why I didnt come out to dinner—I said "Keep still"—he said he never told him a word about it—I said "Do keep still" he grabed a broom stick and jumped up and down and said he didn't have to keep still

Well after the men had gone I went out and got my dinner of course Brother Wever came in before I got through—he said I might just as well have come out to dinner before for he had never intended to tell old Baily any thing about it—I guess he felt kind of cheap when he found he realy had teased me some.

I got the fife out this morning & let Brother Wever try it—he did pretty well for the first time

Well this is all for now I may write more later—yours ever

Bess

P.S. I received letters from Lona Brown and grandma yesterday—Lona has a fellow now by the name of Mr W*m* Dixon and seems to think she is the whole thing now while grandma is much worried on account of not hearing from you folks for over two weeks and it seems so very long—Sylvester, Keneth, and Vivian each wrote her a nice letter at Xmas time and she has just received some splendid pictures of them—How nice!

Mrs Wever has returned and says that Mrs Miller is better Doesnt it beat all how she gets better and worse?

By By—Bess.

I'll write to Grandma soon.

1. Another name for the game of Jacks.

. . . .

JANUARY 27, 1906 TENNANT, IOWA

To J. Olney Corey, Walnut, Iowa

Dear Bid,—Was much pleased to receive your letter and the next time you feel like roasting me for not writing just figure up and see how many letters you owe me

That must have been a stem winder of an exam you took or what was the matter?—Been bluffing? or taking conceit medicine? or wasn't it as bad as you thought?

So you have been walking to school with the Koeppe girls well I don't guess you have to shorten your long graceful strides on their account. Say just tell 'em I'll write to them when they answer my last letter

I hope Mrs Copley had a fine visit in Illinois and I should like very much to come down for over Saturday but don't see how I can as I am so very short of money at present. If you will let me know when that

An undated dramatic production at the Walnut school, showing
a blackface character. Original in Walnut Historical Museum.

Oratorical Contest is to be I'll try and get down if I have to hunt up a
fellow as Valerie advises.

Hazel Lodge must have been trying to take you down a peg. Who
is *Ret*? Lauretta? Well if it is I think that sounds pretty familiar on so
short an acquaintance. Why Bert called me Bess the other evening for
the first time and he looked just as though he expected to get hit but
of course he didn't

Our entertainment turned out fine. The two little *"niggers"* *"took"*
well. Our program was pronounced a success and the Co. Supt. of
schools Mr. Luxford talked to us a while after the program.

The Co. Supt. visited my school two weeks ago Friday—it was examination day and Oh! you aught to have seen things.

The Saturday after our entertainment we spent the evening out and just had a fine time. There was quite a crowd of young folks and we played games and lunched on popcorn and cake. — I had the satisfaction of being *the one* that is I was courted on the *east side* and *west side* at the same time. Say its fun but. I don't like it so very well.

Well that same evening Mrs Miller went to bed not feeling very well and the next Monday the doctor gave her up but she got better any way — she has been given up about six times since but is much better now and they say she will pull through alright. I sat up with her the night of Jan *9th* and Ida came for me the next evening so I have been staying at Wever's ever since. We just have lots of fun since Mrs Miller got better

Say what size of shoes do you wear I've made a pair of slippers — they're tens and they look awful big — Ida said to send one of them to Paulie for a cradle but I just know they wouldn't have room for it. I made them for you and if you can make use of them I'll send them to you if you says so but just tell me whether to ship them by express or freight — Ida says to tell you she thinks they aught to be sent by freight and she say to tell you that *paw* and his son are to be here for dinner

She has just said something more but says not to put that down but it wasn't any thing about you

I let Ida read your letter do you care?

Can you hear Gertie grinding coffee? She wants to know

Ida says to tell you I've got to get up and move the stove.

Ida says to tell you you don't need to read all this cause "I was just ateasing you" I suppose ma sends you my letters so you hear all the news from up here any way but you might write a little oftener any way

Mr Wever's are going to ship their cattle today and we're going to have dinner about half after ten.

Bert says tell you we are having awful nice weather and that reminds me that I had a *lovely* sleighride

Ida says you will have to get excused from school to read this and Mrs Wever says tell you I got up early this morning

Good by quick he's coming write soon Yours as ever

Bess

JANUARY 28, 1906 TENNANT, IOWA

To Mrs. E. O. Corey, Elmdale

Dear folks,—Mrs Miller is still improving and we are all well with the exception of bad colds

Mr Wever started to Chicago with the cattle yesterday afternoon (Jan 27) I don't know when he expects to get back

I received a letter from Olney last week—two whole pages and that's a regular *lunker* when its from Bid.

Ida and Mrs Wever went to Shelby yesterday—they mailed five letters for me—one of them the letter I wrote you a week ago today and suppose you will get it in the course of human events. I also sent one to Olney—I don't know what he will think of it. It was just a terror I wrote it out in the kitchen and first Ida told me something to tell him then Gertie then Mrs Wever then Bert.

Oh! say "Vat you tink" Bert called me "Bess" the other evening and he don't want me to call him Mr Wever but I shan't call him Bert so I wont

Mr Wever says he wont be director[1] any more so I suppose I'm out of a school for next spring.

Say what sort of impression is *she*[2] making on our Toadie this winter?

Say ma I never thought of it till the other day but Mrs Wever is just lots like Mrs Stewart and I dont know but I believe she kind of likes me a little now, that is she dont dislike me the way she did and Oh! I'm so glad!

Mr, Mrs Wever and Lee are going down to Oklahoma when Mr. Wever gets back from Chicago

3 P.M.

Well I started this this morning but gave it up as a bad job—guess I can write a little more now though

Mrs Wever went over to see how Mrs Miller is getting along and Ida Gertie and I were out on the south porch reading when all of a sudden Gertie started up and said "Where's Lee?" no one knew and no one had seen him for a long time so Ida and I went on reading and Gertie went hunting—she went around the house calling "Lee" at the top of her voice finely he answered her and she found him in the—and Oh if you could have seen him—his coat, over shoes, shoes, stockings, and pants were strewn around him and he was finishing disrobing as swiftly as possible. Gertie gathered him and his wearing apparal up and brought them in and placed them (Jan 30) in the middle of the floor and we all stood around and laughed till we almost cried.

Say if you want to send me some message at any time you can phone to Eshers south of Harlan who have the Farmers Mutual and the other phone also and they can phone to me at Wever's and it wont cost you one cent

Must close in haste as ever

Bess

1. Director of the school.

2. There are initials in the margin here that look like "V. H." so this may refer to Valerie Harris.

. . . .

FEBRUARY 6, 1906 TENNANT, IOWA

To Mrs. E. O. Corey, Elmdale

Dear Ma,—Mrs Miller was better for some time but last Saturday afternoon and evening she was worse again. it was her heart this time and they thought sure she was going but i[t] got better again and is still improving.

Last Thursday evening at supper Ida answered the phone and said I was wanted. I couldn't think who on earth would be after wanting me and Brother Wever said it was George S[te]wart I said "It isn't eather," he said it was and I asked him how he knew so much about it and they said he had been at home all day alone and had *hung on* and knew all about it but he didn't know quite as much as he thought. It was Sarah. They've had the phone most a month but didn't know I was at Wevers till I wrote Sarah.

Sarah wanted me to come up Friday evening and stay over till Sunday with her for as Andrew and Belle were hooked together Jan 31 (Wednesday) and George was out taking care of Andies stock till he got home from his honey moon she would be alone or have to hunt up some one to stay with her. I went to Tennant Friday evening after school and went up on the evening train. Sarah came down to meet me but she came one way and I went up another so we missed each other and when I got there she was a block and a half away.

After supper we went to revival meeting. We stoped for Miss Wilson. Saturday we didn't get up very early and it was about half after ten when we got the work done and about that time George and one of the other boys came in with a couple of loads of cobs so Sarah hurried up dinner and I went after the mail. After dinner we went down town I saw Lida Smith and her mother, also Mrs M— oh what is her name its Hattie Hilderbrand that used to be and Magnus Peterson, Pauline Peterson and Dr Hoyt and several others.

The Stewart boys had to go out to their farms again so Sarah and I was going to spend the evening with the Croft girls but Ida Croft phoned in that she was out in the country so we didn't go.

Sunday morning we went to church and after dinner I took the train for Tennant. Mary Stewart was on the same train so I had company Mary and I went to church in Tennant. I got to meet the new married folks.

I got home a little after sun down. I didn't think it was very cold but I most froze one ear—it feels as if it had been chewed and looks that way too

Well the folks are about ready to start so I must close.

Say never mind writing I'll get along alright and I know how busy you are

Yours As Ever

Bess

. . . .

FEBRUARY 15, 1906 TENNANT, IOWA

To Mrs. E. O. Corey, Elmdale

6:45 A.M.

Dear Ma,—Well breakfast is over and as some one will have to go to Tennant today to take the cream I'll write you a little though the last letter I wrote is not yet mailed.

Feb 9th, Tues. Mrs Miller was worse then she was better Wed—worse Thurs better Fri worse Sat. the same till yesterday then worse again the doctor and most every one else has given up hope and most of the Miller family seem to care very little whether she recovers or not for if she don't "Pop can get another one." Though I hope he never will after the care he has taken of this one or rather the care he has *not* taken of her

I was in to see her last evening she just recognized me and that was all and can't hear now unless they just yell at her. They lanced the swelling on her neck some days ago and removed about half a cup of matter. They have to wash it out every day and have to use disinfectants and then they say its dangerous

Monday when I wrote to you and Chall I think I told you it was raining well Monday evening it turned colder and we had a blizard all day Tues.—don't know what you folks had. They wouldn't let Gertie go to school but I went any way—had to follow the fence and then it wasn't any too safe. I went early and had the stove red hot before half past eight. The three Miller boys came and that is all the school I had. They had taken some of their books home the evening before and had learned their reading and spelling so we hurried through and got out about eleven I got to Wevers about half after eleven and I couldn't have gone a quarter of mile farther to have saved my life and if I had attempted to cross the ploughing I wouldn't be writing to you now I dont think. When I got here my clothes from my legging tops to my waist were wet through and getting stiff so I had to change every dud I had on. I'm alright now though.

Yesterday we opened our Valentine box. It was chuck full—every one was remembered—I got fifteen I believe it was. About a dozen of them were from my pupils and three were from outsiders—one from that *interested mamma* who wrote me the note. I tell you but its a *honey*. I bet you and the boys would feel like making things buzz if you could see it. She fixed it up so I couldn't help but know who it was from and then she had brass enough to call me up last night over the phone to find out how Mrs Miller was. You see she is just set on having a racket with me but perhaps she will get left.

Last night Will Dau stayed after school about fifteen minutes just to show me his Valentines and look at mine. Willie is my bestest big boy. He is the only person who has seen my pet Valentine and Oh! my! but he fired up when he saw it. He said he didn't see what they wanted to send such things just to hurt peoples feelings for.

Miss Edith is just Mary Copley Hummer over again only she doesn't use quite such bad language

It is getting late so must close and remain
Your Daughter
Bess

. . . .

FEBRUARY 2[3], 1906[1] TENNANT, IOWA

To Mrs. E. O. Corey

Dear Ma,—Well I reckon you must have received a letter or two from me since the one you wrote the 15*th.*

Oh, thats alright, your guying me about the writing only next time please remember that *what's written goes further than whats said*

My ink is neather too thick nor too deep and if I don't use it all up in writing *this* I've about nine other letters that aught to be written— some of them have been waiting a month or two or longer than that I guess.

I received another Walnut paper[2] yesterday—read it all through already. When I finished reading it I let it slip down and I sat there thinking and pretty soon I was brought back to this world with a bump by hearing Gertie exclaim in an irritated tone "I do wish she would quit sending her those papers she just reads them through and sets around and studys for two or three days." Well you see I was just thinking about that land—I suppose part of the old home will be sold before I see it again. Has J. C. C.—[3] put in a bid yet? I was just think- ing he would likely make an offer for the benefit of himself and sisters thinking if he could get the land for no great price it might further some of his plans for the future when we older children are settled and well out of the way. Vat you tink?.

Last Saturday I sewed the forenoon and in the after noon we all curled our hair and when I curl my hair again tell me about it wont you? Why the kinks aren't out of it yet. When we got our hair curled we all went for a sleigh ride and went over to Millers for a little while—brought my trunk home with us.

Last Sunday we all went up to Ida's Uncle Sams[4] to take her cousin Edith home—I had a fine time. Edith was here just a week and if she had been here just about another one I would just hate the sight of Bert Wever that's what I would. they called him paw and me maw and most teased the life out of us—me any way.

Mrs McK__ made up her mind if she quarreled with me she would have to do all the quarreling so she thought she would try something else. Last Monday the McK. children came in and I spoke to them as usual—I noticed a grin on Nell's face and couldn't help thinking there was a "nigger in the fence"—well they set around with their wraps on for a while till some one asked them if they couldn't take off their things and stay awhile. then they said no they were going home as soon as they got their books. They waited till almost school time then packed up and left shaking the mud off their heels as [they] went. They have given us no excuse that I've heard of excepting that they didn't want to go to school to me any more but I guess every one knows it was just because they couldn't run the school The children are good enough but their ma————!!!!!!!!!!

Last Tuesday afternoon Margaret [Sorenson] came up for the Miller boys—their mamma was dead—died at fifteen minutes after three Before the Miller boys were out of sight half the pupils were crying so I dismissed them though it was just half after three. Mr Miller and Willie were at the sale so Maggie sent Walter after them— I went down to Millers and stayed till Mr Miller came home then I had the job of sending the word to their relatives and as some of them had just received letters from Maggie saying that Mrs Miller was better it was quite a shock to them. I had to send several messages and arange for some of them to meet in Avoca to make arrangements. My! it was the hardest work I've done this year. I was sweating like a bucher when I got through

Tuesday evening I called up Mr Plumb and after a little talk decided to dismiss school for the rest of the week you see the school house is so near Millers the children wouldn't study if they came and it might bother Millers so as I had Thanksgiving day and Xmas day I will just have an extra week to teach onto the end of the term so my school wont be out till Mar 16th. Im sorry cause I've planned so much on being home by your birthday if possible but I can't now.

Wednesday morning Ida and I went over to Millers and helped for a while then after dinner us girls were going over to Tennant to take the cream and brother Wever insisted on leaving the cream so he could go too. We went in the double buggy and be *darned* if we didn't spring the hind axial. Oh you need not be so shocked at the language I just used and if you could hear some of the language storeys, and songs that I do you would wonder at my using such mild terms and really they dont do the subject justice

We went to the funeral yesterday fornoon. it was sad to see those children when they realized that they were looking at their mamma for the last time. just think—eight of them and the eldest younger than our Toadie. I didn't know any of the relatives except Mrs Peter Nelson.

We didn't go to Avoca—didn't dare to—every time we hit a bump that axial would crack a little more and by the time we got home the wheels nearly touched the seat.

I spent yesterday afternoon in cleaning and mending some of my clothes and could put in another day or two at it. I aught to go to Harlan tomorrow on the morning train to attend teachers meeting all day but I dont know whether I will or not. The frost is out of the ground in places and the walking may not be bad. Sarah[5] wanted me to come up last week to attend the Y.M.C.A.[6] lectures, they were to have speakers from N.Y. Nebraska and some from Iowa. I couldn't go on account of the roads and other things.

Ida's folks haven't written when they were coming back but they will surely come soon.

Brother Wever is going to Tennant some time today to take the cream so I will have a chance to get this mailed

I guess this is about all for now but I'll read your letter over and see—No I haven't heard from Olney for quite a while—my last letter must have insulted him or he is in a rush or perhaps it's a little of both.

It is Mr Henry Esher south of Harlan who has the two phones—did you get the message I sent you that way?

Yes, I bet you were wrathy about the way the little Dane kept school. I'm curious to know about the war between England and Denmark.

You didn't tell me about the second apprasial.

Ask Paul if he wants me to come home

Yours—Bess.

P.S. I enclose a letter to Ethel from one of my language class.[7]

1. The letter itself says February 2, but the envelope is dated February 23, and since the letter discusses Mrs. Miller's death, it must have been written after the February 15 letter (CMW).

2. The weekly newspaper the *Walnut Bureau*, which the Corey family usually forwarded to Bess.

3. J. C. Corey.

4. This visit, to Sam McKeighan, was reported in the *Shelby County Republican* on February 22, 1906 (CMW).

5. Probably Sarah Stewart.

6. There was a Y.M.C.A. in Harlan at this time.

7. No enclosure was found with the letter (CMW).

· ·

MARCH 3, 1906 TENNANT, IOWA

To Mrs. E. O. Corey

Dear Mamma,—Vell vat you tink of this weather? Olney home yet? Guess I'll write him a strictly buisness letter as soon as I get some of my other business straightened out.

Last Tuesday evening little Edward Miller was knocked down by a horse and was not at school the rest of the week I was down to see him two or three times and am glad to say that he is improving and perhaps be able to come to school next week.

Another one of my big boys quit school last evening to commence farm work next week. He was my bestest big boy. He staid awhile after the rest had gone and when he said good bye I said perhaps I wouldn't see him again and he said "Oh I hope you will, maybe I'll come down some time." I hope he will for I know the boys would like him and he would just do almost any-thing for me. I wonder if Fuller remembers him—that big homely Dutch boy named Willie Dau.

Two of Ida's cousins were down to spend the evening last Monday and one of them hardly took his eyes off me till after supper—I just felt like throwing my knife and fork at him.

Mr Wevers hired man arrived Thursday. His name is Carl Jensen and Oh but he is great in almost every sence of the word.

I've got my weight up to 210 again and just can't raise it an ounce Perhaps I can before I go home though for the folks just butchered yesterday and now we will have lots of fresh meat.

Say ma Brother Wever has got heart trouble

My school closes Wednesday March 14*th* and you can send one of the boys up for me and my baggage *Saturday Mar. 17* for I am not going to apply for this school again—am going to try to get a school nearer home

I dont think I will have more than a week at home and I expect you will be mighty glad of it before you get through with it for I am getting to be the most uneasy mortal you ever saw Ida says she don't believe I could keep still if I had to and I'm almost afraid she is right. One evening I read just as long as I could stand it and I just jumped up and started to do something else as if my life depended on it — Brother Wever was laying on the sofa and he sat up and exclamed, "Good Lord do you very often move that fast?"

Goodness me but money is a slippy thing even when it isn't greased—I don't believe I'll have ten dollars left when I get through here but then I'll have my buggy paid for any way—I sent E. O. Armstrong a money order a week ago Wednesday but have received no receipt as yet so I dont know whether it reached him or not.

My but I've a lot of things to tell you when I get home—some of them would take to much room some are unwritable—about Xmas presents and the like.

Little Frank Buckley is here on a visit, he was home sick last evening.

Well Mrs Wever and Ida are cutting up the meat and they made me clear out so I guess I better close

I've got to make my bed yet and I aught to go down to Trottner's and Dau's.

I'm not going to do any more washing till I get home so I'll have to borrow some of yours while all of mine are in the wash

Wevers are breaking colts so it is quite interesting around here

The boys wont ever be able to tease me any more for it will be tame after what I'm used to here but it isn't as bad as when the folks were away

Well I must close and remain as ever—Bess

Elisabeth F Corey

Tennant Ia

I'm going to town with Ida this afternoon though I aught to be sewing.

I may not write you another letter—just save up the rest till I get home

So Long—Bess.

You know that collar that Flora Koeppe gave me well I gave the cuffs to Gertie and she wants the collar to match so if you will please send it to me I'll be much obliged and make it square with you sometime. E. F. C.

MARCH 6, 1906 TENNANT, IOWA

To Mr. J. Olney Corey, Elmdale

To J. Olney, H. Fuller, Robert L., Ethel G., Challenge R, and Paul F Corey of Marne Iowa

:—I the undersigned give you authority, herewith to present to your mother Margaret M. Corey, Mar. 11, 1906 (her birthday) the top buggy which you will find in the buggyshed on the E. O. Corey estate. The same is owned by me having purchased same of E. O. Armstrong, Marne, Ia. November 13, 1905.

There now!!! I'm rid of it and *now* if it gets its bones broken I wont have to pay the doctor bills.

I ask as a special favor that in the future you never mention my name in connection with that buggie or refer to me as the former owner of it

Yours Truly

E. F. Corey, Tennant, Iowa

MARCH 28, 1906 TENNANT, IOWA

To Mrs. E. O. Corey, Elmdale

Dear Mamma,—Well this is Wed. evening and I will try to write you a little letter of fifteen pages or about that.

Well as I do not know how much Olney told you I will begin at the very first—Our ride Saturday was uneventful save Olneys playing teeter board over the back of the buggy seat for exercise. We hardly knew where we were at when we got into this part of the country part of the road I had been on once and part of it I had never been on at all—We stoped at Shaffers to inquire the road to Browns and when we got to Browns we found that Mr Grauel had spoken to Shaffers about board for me.

Brown's were very good to us and we had the pleasure of meeting Miss May Brown who is a teacher in the H.H.S. There are only two of the Brown boys at home Lewis and Will the insane one. Will used to teach school before he went insane but the last two school[s] he tried to teach the pupils all left before two weeks were up on account of his queer actions—they were afraid of him. Shortly after he quit teaching they took him to the asylum but as there was no help for him and as he was not dangerous they brought him home six months or a year ago. His eyes had a queer look in them but that was all I noticed about him that was queer. I'm so glad Olney didn't know any thing about him befor going there it might have given him *two tree nerves*[1]

Well I think Mr Brown will make a good director but I think he's something of a crank—begging his pardon

Yes and they got me the raise in wages that they half promised but which I did nont expect. I now receive $38.00 which is more than any other teacher in this t'w'p will receive this spring

And Mr Wever has made the Tennant people think that they were getting something *great* by getting me for teacher and of course they are getting something *great* in one sence of the word

You know Mr Wever resigned so Mr McKeighan hired the teacher so Wevers don't have to board her and no one else will and she is still looking for board some two or three miles from school. I'm sorry for her for if she is the kind of girl the folks here say she is she will be sure to have a deal of trouble befor she gets through with it. Her younger brother goes to school to me and seems to be a nice quiet kind of boy.

You know I had a queer kind of feeling in my bones[2] about that Elsie Neugent? Well she tried awful hard to get this school and her folk are awfuly out with Mr Grauel and others for working so hard for me. Her brother Pierce is coming clear down here to school and he isn't even in this township. I guess he is a good enough boy but he is a queer chicken and quite mischievos

There were fourty or more pupils enrolled last winter but several familys have moved away so I have only twenty five as yet although there are several who have not started on account of sickness.

A man in Tennant told the pupils if they would put the new teacher out doors he would give them a nickel's worth of candy apiece. Today they tried to persuade me to let them do it by promising me half of the candy all round.

Oh yes Hazel Reynolds cousin Edith Graves wanted this school too I have eight pupils who want to take the final examination in May so that makes *heaps* of work for me to do.

I have had my mail twice this week have received your card and one from Aunt Jennie and also a letter from Ida Wever.

Ida says that "Mr Grauel and Mr Brown are going to stand to your back (for mercy sake don't fall over on them) and they are going to have *order*." She said that Gertie was *teakettled* to get the collar but when she found I had that letter of hers she-she-she-she-she—and the worst of it is I can't find that letter high or low and I've looked through all my papers and books

I most forgot to tell you about my boarding place. I like it just fine I have a heated room of[f] the sitting room. it is a snug *homelike* little room 3 x 6 x 9 ft with two windows and furnished with a bed a dresser two chairs two rows of well filled books and my trunk and grip. I find that by setting one chair out side I can *turn clear around* at the risk of tearing the lace curtain, upsetting the pin tray and pulling most of the clothes off the hooks. And after several experiments I found that by climbing to the farther side of the bed and raising the window I can with much care remove both shoes without much danger to the miror and without loseing my garters in the wash bowl.

The feed here is great—right up to Grandma's or Mrs Copleys or yours

Mrs Shaffer is an old friend and schoolmate of Anna and Belle Stewart—she and Belle were always the closest of friends and Belle was down and stayed several days with her just a short time befor she was married.

Well I guess I had better close for now and remain as ever yours with love—Bess

1. The last word could also be "never."

2. Bess felt that she had a streak of psychic awareness now and then. Distinct "feelings" came upon her unexpectedly and unannounced, usually to inform her about something dire that was going to happen.

. . . .

APRIL 2, 1906 TENNANT, IOWA

To Mr. J. Olney Corey, Elmdale

Dear Brother,—Did you get Aprilfooled yesterday? I didn't but know some one who did.

I got through my first week of school pretty well. Pierce Neugent has quit to work on the section but as Walter Hack and Walter Pingel have started in, my school is still growing

I've sure struck a jolly crowd but my!! what a tease Mr Shaffer is!!!
Why he's worse than Ida Wever.

I received a letter from Alma Johansen and also one from Ida
Wever. Ida said Gertie was teakettled to get the collar but I guess she
nearly boiled over that letter of hers. of course she knows I just took
it for *meaness* as Rob used to say and the worst of it is I can't find
hide nor hair of that letter among my things I just looked them clear
through. If you can find it any where please send it to me and there is
a paper in the machine drawer with Ethels measure on it please copy
it off and send it to me for I happen to recomember that I never sent
her measure to Mrs Wheeler.

I'm so glad mamma got Mary for a few days I can sleep better now.

I wrote a letter last week and Mr Shaffer went up to Tennant to
mail it for me and of course he forgot it entirely then we all went
up Saturday evening and I forgot it so Mr Shaffer took it up Sunday
morning and *mailed* it

Oh! say do you know Teddy? No I guess I didn't write any thing
about him last time. He is a lovely old maid gentleman of Tennant
who told my pupils that he would give them a nickels worth of candy
apiece if they would throw the new schoolma'am out doors. May the
rats get his ornery picture if he didn't come mighty near making
things *pleasant* fore me. Mrs Shaffer went for him today and asked
him what he ment by putting such notions into the childrens heads
and he laughed and said he knew they couldn't

Yesterday *Paw* and *Maw* Walmer were down so I've had the plea-
sure(?)[1] of meeting Mrs Walmer at last and when I was out of hearing she says "Why how awful quiet the teacher is" she thought I had
so *very* little to say and Mrs Shaffer said she felt like telling her that
I realy couldn't say *much* under the circumstances. We all went to
church Sunday and I believe I knew half of the people there—Ida,
Gertie and Bert were there and Uncle Sam and Edith and oh I don't
know how many more I knew.

I most forgot to tell you. Mr Grauel come near having to take a
licking for what he did to help me. I watched my chance Saturday
evening to thank him for his kindness and he told me about it. He
said when Eshers sent him my phone message Neugents were hanging on[2] and they thought Mr Grauel was working for me and against
Elsie and he Mr Neugent was going to make Mr Grauel a hot time but
I guess he didn't

Mr Shaffer just got back from Tennant and said he wouldn't have been gone so long but Crysless or what ever his name is had to stop him to ask about the schoolma'am.

Say vat you think some of the girls around here are wearing black sateen shirts for waists they just let them blouse over and it was quite a while before I caught on to it that they were just mens shirts. Just wait till I get home again and you will *need* "to keep your shirt" on

Well its getting late so you will have to share this up with the rest so long

Your Sister

Bess.

Write soon

P.S. Mrs Hamler came to me after church and said if she could help me in any way to let her know as she thought it was better when parents & teacher worked together

1. The question mark is Bess's (CMW).

2. In other words, listening in to the party line on the phone.

. . . .

APRIL 8, 1906 TENNANT, IOWA

To Mrs. E. O. Corey, Elmdale

Dear Mamma, — Hello how you commin? How long did Mary stay? How much of your work did you get caught up? How's the weather and the farm work? How's school down there? Are you over your cold yet?

I've had all kinds of a time this week. If I can get a *"First Grade"* this summer I'll teach it out and then go home and help my ma if she'll let me. Guess we can get along if we cant agree.

I guess there is about the same number of kickers in each neighborhood and you know how hard I always took being criticised for doing what I *know* is right. Of course the harder the cranks turn the more friends it makes for me but its unpleasant just the same.

I tell you what! there is work enough for two teachers here. I work as hard as I can dig from eight o'clock till six and then have two or three hours work to do on Saturday and then there is so much going on it keeps me jumping I tell you I'm going some these two weeks

I went down to Browns Tuesday evening and Mabel and I went to

Tennant Wednesday eve Thursday evening Mr and Mrs Shaffer were over to Tatmans and didn't get home till eleven. I trimed a box for the social while they were gone. It was shaped like a house with white tisue paper put on in tucks for siding and the three windows and one door had green frames. the roof was shingled with brown wrapping paper. It was real pretty and so different from all the rest of the boxes.

Friday evening I went to the Social in Tennant with Miss May Brown and her brother Lewis. Had a fine time. Four of the Miss Eshers were there and I got quite well acquainted with two of them. I also met Miss Morris who teaches No 1. I planned so much on seeing Ida and Bert but was dissapointed. I was so glad that Uncle Sam McKeighan got my box for I was afraid "Crazy John" would get it.

We were invited up to Uncle Georges for today but it rained so yesterday, last night and this morning that we had to give it up.

I have to dress "*sweller*" now I live just half a mile out of town and am *quality folks*. I got me a new cap and gloves that can be worn all the year around and enough ribbon like the scrap enclosed to make a bow for my hair and a neck ribbon that goes twice around my neck and ties in a—what is it? *foreign*hand or a *fourinhand*.[1] You can't tell much about it from the little piece but it is really the prettiest ribbon I ever saw.

There is a family of Longneckers living some two or three miles from here and Mrs L— told Mr Shaffer to ask me if I was acquainted with the Browns and Hadleys near Walnut. That they were relatives of hers and she thought she had heard tell of *me*. Please write and tell me who she is.

Well it has quit raining and the sun is out blazing hot—I gess it wont stay clear long.

Mr Shaffer was telling the other evening about an old dutchman who used to come home drunk and say "Ma you old fool I like you" then *he* got to saying it to tease Mrs Shaffer and Glen who is five was playing on the floor and pretty quick he said "Pa you old fool I like you" His pa looked as though he would like to sell out for about two cents and a half.

It is 2:10 P.M. Mrs Kohl and children are here and I've "dressed up," put on my black skirt and white waist with black spots which I find fits first rate without any changeing. having made myself as uncomfortable as possible I have locked myself in my room to write letters and work up some outlines for the eighth grade.

I believe I'm like Margaret and would rather stay at home and "Raise chickens, make garden and slop hogs" than teach school.

10:15 P.M. Mrs Shaffer was a hanging on this evening and heard some more about *"this teacher."* Most every one liked Miss Stanley[2] and as Mr Brown (begging his pardon) is an old crank I haven't an easy place by any means. Don't worry about me for as long as I do what I *know* is right I'll have *some* good friends.

Yours Ever—Bess

[Written on top of page 3:] P.S. I have more friends than enemies and among my friends are Grauels, Bishops and Hamler the Druggest—the best and most influencial people in Tennant

[Enclosure: Preserved with this letter is a slip of the silk-like fabric Bess describes, a light golden tan in color, carrying a high sheen.]

1. The knot used in tying a man's tie was in the past called a four-in-hand knot.

2. This could be Carrie Stanley, the previous teacher.

. . . .

APRIL 11, 1906 TENNANT, IOWA

To Mrs. E. O. Corey, Elmdale

Dear Mamma,—Mr Shaffer went up to Tennant Monday evening and recomembered to get my mail—I was so glad to get your letter. Mrs Shaffers brother was here when he returned and we all didn't get to bed till half after ten.

Yesterday morning Sadie Barret 'phoned for Mrs Shaffer to come over to sit with Mrs Tatman who has been ill since a week ago Sunday and is not expected to live long so she went for all day—after school Mabel and I did dinner dishes, got supper and did supper dishes then the children went down to Kohls and Mr Shaffer and I went over to Tatman's. Shaffers came home and I stayed. Mrs Tatmans trouble seems to be something fierce. (Epileptic Paralises). she has no power over her left limbs and some nights they had to have four or five persons there as it took three at a time to keep her in bed. Last night Mr George Slaughter and I sat up *all* night & Mr Tatman sat up with us till midnight then Miss Tatman got up and stayed up till morning.

Mr Slaughter is a widower with twin sons about ten years of age—his wife died of consumption seven years ago—he and his children live with a married brother not far from here and Mr Slaughter is acquainted with Mr T. Kite and Mr George Copley from near Walnut and he's fine I tell you what!!! most as nice as Joe Stewart a little bit some once more already yet—how you like that. !!?!??!!!!!

(Mr Shaffer say to tell you that he is going to help me a whole lot in fact he is going to hunt me up a fellow.)

Mr Slaughter went home about five this morning and I got home about seven and took a nap before going to school. Its most half after eight so I'll ring off pretty soon and go to roost.

I suppose when the ceiling fell in you felt like Chicken-Little.

Sena missed connections something like her letter didn't she?

I'm glad Mr C— got down and you all got things straightened out alright but can't see why both boys went to the train with him.

Rob is doing well to milk seven cows if he did it with out bawling.

Wishing Olney a happy birthday I will close and remain as ever Elizabeth F Corey

PS got the buggy cleaned yet? I've thought of it so many times I'm sorry we took it but the other was so uncomfortable.

· ·

APRIL 22, 1906 TENNANT, IOWA

To Mrs. E. O. Corey, Elmdale

Dear mamma,—Your card was received Friday—I hope this will find you well again.

I suppose you have felt as though I had forgotten you because I havent written oftener but you can always take it for granted that if you dont hear from me there must be some good reason for it.

I tell you I've had a week of it—Sunday we all went down to Shelby—we took dinner at Green's so I made the acquaintance of Mrs Shaffer's father and mother and also her brother John and his wife and children then about four o'clock we went over to Shaffers so I met Mr Shaffers father and mother also his sister Blanch her husband and little daughter Florence Elizabeth Green. also the Fouts family. We got home before it got very late—it wasn't dark yet. Somehow that evening I just felt as though there was something wrong and Oh! how I wished I was home and when Mr Shaffer laughed at me for being homesick I threw Glens shoes at him, hiting him with both, then hastily retired.

I had been wanting two of my little pupils to go back[1]—had explained it to them so they could see that they would gain by it in the end and then Monday morning they came to school each saying that her *paw said* that he would keep her out of school before he would have her put back so Monday evening I went to see their folks at the first place Mrs. Wm. H— said she agreed with me but her husband did not but she would talk it over with him then her little girl went with me to the other place to show me the road and the other woman treated me *so very nice* and said it would be just all right but when I got home I told Mrs Shaffer that she was nice to me but I had my doubts about how it was now already so soon and at the Aid Society Mrs Lawson, whose daughter was there while I was there, said that Nina said it was something wonderful the way she talked about me before I was out of sight even. well the next day the two little girls went back and Mrs Wm. H— was at Mrs Shaffers all day and told her all about it, she said that she explained it to her husband and he gave in and was satisfied then he went down town and saw the other little girls father who was cussing the teacher to beat everything telling just what he told me using a great deal of —?—!—?—!!!!— — — kind of language and that got Mr Wm H— all stired up again and he came home a swearing and told about it and his wife said she didn't believe the man ever saw me at all and the little girl spoke up and said that he wasn't home yet when we were there then her pa almost flew to pieces he was so mad at the other fellow for lieing to him but he has cooled of and *thats* another family in my favor which makes eight for, four against and one or two that are neither. then I dont think I told you that the Pingle children (four)[2] quit this school because the teacher didn't "help them enough" and they were going down to No 5 but the teacher told them to go to their own school and to never come back there again so as near as I can make out Mr Pingle went to Harlan to see the Superintendant, hoping to make me what he would call a H— of a time and Wednesday afternoon just as I was hearing the first reader class after dinner I looked up and there stood Mr Luxford beside me. Goodness but I was startled. Well he stayed till five oclock that evening and gave me all the suggestions and pointers that I was going up to Harlan Saturday after—Mr Pingle came in about Recess and stayed till after the Supt went home—well Mr Luxford told him to send his children back to school in the morning and they came. My but you would snort if you knew some of the things he said to me after Mr Luxford went but I will have to leave that to *tell* as it is *unwritable*. Every thing is going smooth enough now. Next Friday is Arbor day and we are to give a program so I will have another busy week of it though they are all busy enough.

Monday afternoon Mrs Shaffer got me the gingham to make Ethel a shirtwaist suit like Mabels I worked at it evenings and finished it Saturday morning all but the button holes then we went down to Shelby and I finished it and sent it so Ethel would get it on her birthday. I also got the tie and hair ribbons to match it and will enclose them. the tie is to be worn in a big bow—and there is enough for two good hair ribbons. Do write and tell me how it fits for of course a good deal of it was guess work. I just hope the neck isn't too large, the armholes to small, the sleaves to long, the waist to short, the tucks to deep, and the skirt to narrow.

I got me a hat in Shelby—a pretty though very simple little hat and every one says it fits and looks just fine and makes me look taller. It is almost round and quite high and has a bunch of geranium leaves and buds (pink) and a little white ribbon Its a hat that wont look out of place anywhere or with any dress which is just the kind I like and think you will too.

As I forgot to bring Robberts dictionary I purchased one Saturday, a little dandy some what larger than Rob's.

I've lost your card and can[t] find it any where.

I almost forgot to tell you but I heard Grandma Shaffer talking about me she said "Why she just seems like one of the family to me she is large like Blanch and her name is *Florence Elisabeth* too" We took dinner at Grandma Shaffer's yesterday and Blanch and her husband and the baby were here all day today. Mr Shaffer's twin brother and his whole family stopped here a few minutes this morning and were here to supper this evening. They want me to come over some Friday evening and stay till Sunday evening and Ethel Rink wants me to come down to McGill for Saturday and Sunday and I promised Aunt Jennie one and I received a letter from Ida Wever Monday and she wants me to come over there she says she doesn't get to go any where any more and she was about as blue as she could be I guess. she said she felt like a line in a song "The day goes by Like a shadow o'er the heart"

I *just must* write to her

We put down the sitting room carpe[t] last evening after supper—I blistered my knuckles and then knocked one blister off this morning but dont tell the boys cause they will think I'm soft

Did I say any thing in my last letter about a new ring it had three opals and four diamonds set this way [a small drawing with 3 large circles and 4 smaller ones appears in the letter here] Oh how they sparkled but I've given it back already so soon

Well I must close for now and if you dont feel like writing or haven't time just have one of the boys drop me a card

Yours As Ever

Bess.

[written at the top of page 1:] I weigh 209 lbs. Ida Wever says I write Rainbow letters cause there are streaks of all colors in them.

[Enclosure: a note for Ethel:]

To Ethel, from her little sister Bessie, for her Birthday April 23. May you have many happy birthdays.

April 22, 1906, Elisabeth F. Corey Tennant Iowa

1. Presumably she means to go back to a lower grade in the school.

2. The Pingels had fifteen children altogether, although most of them were grown by this time. Since Bess mentions Walter, the others who quit were probably Lillie, Herbert, and Franz, as those were the other three youngest children. The father, Peter Pingel, was involved in education at the county level, so it would be interesting to know the story behind his feud with Bess (CMW).

. . . .

APRIL 29, 1906 TENNANT, IOWA

To Mrs. E. O. Corey, Elmdale

Dear Mamma,—yours of the 26th was received yesterday—was very glad to get it was so worried for fear Ethels dress would not fit and if I had that blue goods I could soon finish it.

This last week was a bad one we had to get up a program for Arbor Day and had just a week so of course everything seemed crowded then Thurs. afternoon "vat you tink" nine Harlan High School girls walked in and stayed an hour or so. John Morgans were moving away from Harlan and they went down to the train to see them of[f] and were then going to school but the train was late and did not leave till about eleven oclock so what should they do but come on down to Tennant and phone up to their folks that they would return on the evening train. I suppose they came out to visit the school to pass away time. I had never met any of them before but had heard of Helen Swift and Beatrice Byers Some of them behaved nicely and some of them (ahem) well they were just a crowd of girls out for a lark—one senior six juniors and two sophmores. But can you imagine how I felt when those nine strange girls walked in?

Then Friday we did our gardening in the forenoon gave our program at 2 oclock and got home early. We had six visitors.

Yesterday I made my brown waist and got it all finished and discovered that my trunk is buggie if I aint Today we were all down to Hopkins for all day and had a good time. We all were weighed and I weighed 214 lbs. but how on earth I can gain I don't see.

Mrs Shaffer says for you not to worry if anything should happen or if I should be unable to write that she will write to you or let you know.

Now I'm going to tell you something just to ease my mind but you must not worry cause I'm all right.

Well some how or other I got the feeling that there was some one prowling around so I got so I never went out side the door after night without some one else with me—well night before last I wrote to Mary and Valerie[1] and didn't go to bed till half after ten I believe it was. well there are lace curtains at the windows but they are thin so any one could see through them—I supposed the window shade was down and was undressing when I found my self getting uneasy and feeling as if some one was watching me I glanced at my door but it was closed—I went to my trunk for some thing turning my back to the window when the feeling became so strong I could almost feel my hair rise—by some strange instinct I turned and sprang to the window and drew the shade down exclaiming twice to my self, without knowing why, "There's someone there." I then locked my door, blew out the light, raised the shade carefuly, opened the window quickly and listened. I heard the sound of a stick breaking twice as if some one stepped back quick at the sound of the window. It might have just been some one prowling around but if it is anyone shadowing me I know who it is and am on the alert

My trust in God grows stronger every day. I wish Olney would have another quarterly sent to me.

Tell Fuller it is to bad about the overalls but I didn't have his measure.

What on earth does Robert mean by twisting his name around? Tell him I'd like to turn him down across a chair and use the fire shovel on him

How much corn and how much small grain are the boys going to put in? How many cows are you milking? How is the spring work in general?

Tell Ethel I was glad to get her letter but Mable was dissapointed because she didn't get one too

Ma you just make my feet sweat can't I wear some ones else ring with out a widower or an old batch haveing any thing to do with it.

Mrs Hopkins told Mrs Shaffer to phone down when she found out for sure whether we would come down or not so Saturday evening just for a joke Mrs Shaffer called them up and let me talk just to fool them,—I said "ma said to tell you we all is coming down tomorrow" Mrs Hopkins said "alright come ahead. who is this?" I said it was "ma's bigest girl" we kept it agoing till we all got so tickled we couldn't stand it then Mrs Shaffer finished We had lots of fun over it though. Shaffers introduce me as their "eldest" and consider me their "Bess"

Oh say tell the boys that there is a boy going to school here who is fourteen years old he is a jolly mischievous though very gentlemanly boy who has a taste for music and collecting and also for inventing and drawing—he plays the violin and sings—has started collections of birds egg, foreign coins and pressed flowers. Several years ago when he was still a little boy he hit upon the idea of using wire netting to make a fly-killer and made one for his grandma who found it handy and laughingly told him to get a pattent on it and two years later a young fellow from near there got a patent on that very kind of a fly killer and is now worth thousands of dollars. He is much interested in my brothers and likes to have me tell about them he has heard about the boat and the pond and is fond of boating and when I spoak of his going to see my brothers some time his eyes sparkled and he said "I bet it would be fun." He rides his wheel to and from school

My! it is late! I will close at once Yours As Ever Bess

P.S. I wrote to you last evening but clear forgot to mail the letter so will add a little to it.

It has rained all day today and so of course the children were as full of mischief as they could stick. Vat you tink?!!! Mr Pingle stopped for the children this evening and I ask him how it was and he said "fine." I asked him if he was satisfied he said yes he would not com-

Drawing of a ballgame by one of Bess's students,
mentioned in her letter of April 29, 1906.

plain when things were going so fine so I've conquered the Pingles—
something no other teacher has ever done so have the bells rung, the
horns blown, the tin pans pounded, the fire arms discharged, and
sing all the triumphant songs you know for I've conquered the whole
Pingle tribe. Hurrah!!!!

My how it does rain!! and thunder! and the lightening makes the
phone ring every once in a while

Mabel had to come home before noon she seems about down sick
they are afraid she will have *tonsiletis* (?)

I cut out my "yaller buff" waist tonight and will send you a piece of
it and the one I finished Saturday

I am thinking of going up to Omaha with Bishops some time soon
and might have something done about my hearing if I could afford it
but they say an examination would cost $5 and the treatment would
cost accordingly so I guess that settles it.

Tell Olney to send me Mr Fonda's address perhaps I will get him
to treat me.

Well it is after nine so I will close and rest up for another rainy day
tomorrow—

Yours with love to all—Bess.

This is what Ida Wever calls one of my rainbow letters—it is a little bit of all colors.

[written upside down on page 3:] I will enclose a picture my mischievous boy drew in school time. you cant appreciate it as you would if you knew the players and he didn't get it finished

[Enclosed with letter: 1. The pupil's pencil sketch of seven schoolboys playing baseball at recess time. The game is in progress, the pitcher winding up, the batter at the alert. 2. Folded inside the sketch are snippets of the two cotton fabrics for Bess's planned waists. One is the "yaller buff"—a pleasant shade of tan, the other has a dark brown background on which are printed small white paisley designs.]

1. Probably Mary Lanigan and Valerie Harris. Mary Lanigan was about Bess's age and she taught school nearby.

- -

MAY 7, 1906 TENNANT, IOWA

To Mrs. E. O. Corey, Elmdale

Dear mamma,—Well I'll begin where I left off and I think I left off last Tues. well Tuesday evening I worked on my "yaller buff" waist and Wednesday evening I had a belief of misplaced furnature in my upper story. Thursday I went down to Pingels after school (about a mile and a quarter) and stayed a while, saw their many pretty flowers and the lemon growing on the tree then I walked back to Browns and stayed to supper had a pretty good time. Had intended to get back to Shaffers before dark but Mrs Brown had so many things to talk about and show me that it was dark befor I knew it. I started as soon as I noticed how dark it was getting and just as I started Mr Seward Brown who is visiting there came around the corner of the house and he walked home with me. Oh you need not laugh he's a married man an walked home with me because it isn't safe for a girl to leave there alone after dark.

Friday evening I went to Harlan, just as I was ready to start Mr Brown came along so I rode up with him to Tennant then went on up to Harlan with Mary Stewart—(Anna's sister.) I went up to Aunt Jennies and stayed all night. The next morning I went down town—

the Superintendant was out of town—I went up to see Sarah—got there about ten o'clock and stayed till noon then went to Dunlavys to dinner—went down town again about three or four oclock and Aunt Jennie came down about half an hour later we met Miss Armstrong in Fosters and had quite a talk and when she found I was going up to Stewarts that night she decided to call there in the evening. I also saw Mrs Fish and heard her tell about the earthquake in California which happened while she was there

Aunt Jennie went with me to see Dr Cobb and he examined my head he tested my eyes and ears and examined my throat. he said my eyes were all right but my throat and ears were "*all wrong.*" You know they say that he generally swears at folks and tells them they are all right so perhaps Aunt Jennie will think its something serious because he looked so sober and was so kind and he never swore once the whole while we were there. He said he used to be well acquainted with papa. He gave me something to treat my ears with but said I might have to have my throat treated for sometime befor my hearing would improve. I will do as he said for a while and then if Olney will send me Mr Fonda's address I will write and have him treat me for I think twenty five dollars that way will be better than a hundred and twenty five paid to a *Specialist.* If you should happen to hear some thing of it from Aunt Jennie you need not worry for she may think that its worse than it is.

I went back to Aunt Jennies for supper and then went up to Stewarts for over night. when I got there Curtiss was in bed and George had just got home from the cemetary where he had been all day fixing up the lots and planting flowers. Alice was there and she stayed till George took her home. The next morning we rustled around and Sarah got dinner started before we went to church.

Joe and Andrew and Belle came in but i[t] was near church time and Joe was in his work clothes so he didn't go but all the rest did. then after church Mrs Stewart, Mary, Ellen, Will, Belle, Andrew, Mrs Smith and Lida all came up to dinner and stayed all afternoon.

George took me to the train and I and Mary left for Tennant on the 6:30 and I got out to Shaffers quite a while before dark.

I hope you will pardon the liberty I took in sending you that waist but I did not cut it by my old pattern and when finished I found it too tight in the sholders and short in the sleeves so will be much obliged if you can take it off my hands—if I had had time I would have tacked the collar on and added buttons and button holes but was too busy.

Sarahs eldest brothers eldest son has taken a homestead in S Dakota and wants her to come up, and take one and she wants me to go up and take one too. she says I could clear $1000 in a year up there and I would like to try it. we talk of going up at the end of this term as I will have a week vacation before Summer School commences. It will cost us at least fifty dollars each to file then we can come back here and go up again next Spring and live on it eight months and improve which will cost at least $200 that is counting in the cost of the deed which is $.50 per acre and at the end of a year it will be worth ten or fifteen dollars an acre or more as time goes on—It would be alright *if* I could raise the money nesacessary this Spring for you see I could come back and teach next fall and winter and raise the money for next spring and perhaps I could get a school up there next spring as they say teachers are in great demand in some parts of Dakota. You might talk it over with the boys some time when you have time and see what they think of it—perhaps they could help me raise the money—you know "grub stakes" mean half the profit.

I saw Mr Cullison in Harlan and had a talk with him he said he wasn't going to sell the three fourtys till August any way for fear the purchaser would come on to you for rent. Mr Cullison said he thought I would make a good lawyer and for me to come and study with him—how do you like that.

Oh my how late its getting and I've got to get to school early tomorrow morning.

Mabel sends a letter to Robert in hopes that either Ethel or he will write to her. If he can read all the mischief between the lines he will think its a good one. I'll stake a fiver that he don't kiss Stubbs for her or any other girl

Well so long

Bess

Elisabeth F Corey

Tennant, Ia.

MAY 14, 1906 TENNANT, IOWA

To Mrs. E. O. Corey, Elmdale

Dear mamma,—Last Monday evening I wrote to Ida Wever and Friday I got a letter, or note rather, from her roasting me for not answering her last letter but of course she got the one I wrote when she mailed that one. The note reminded me of that song "It Was The Dutch" for it vas von of dose Dutchies—just a caution so I answered it Friday eve and sent her as good as she gave.

I guess everything is going fine now—it *seems* to be any way. (at school)

Saturday morning I was at the school house by eight o'clock and didn't get back till five minutes to twelve—just worked every minute of the time to—have all of my school work caught up for once but it wont stay there long.

Saturday afternoon Mrs Shaffer, the boys and I went to Tennant—I got your letter and went down to the bank with Mrs Shaffer and read it while she phoned to her sister way up north, then she tried talking to you—said she could hear you just as plain.

I phoned out to Ida from the store and then walked out there and took their mail—It was a little late when I got there but they seemed so glad to see me—Mrs Wever and Ida came clear down to the gate to meet me and you aught to have seen Lee he just came a tearing. I[t] seems so funny to hear them speak about "Bessie" being "home for over Sunday" or about when "Bessie comes home again." Ida and I had a good old visit after we retired—I told her what Mr Cullison said about my making a good lawyer and she said she thought I would make a good judge cause everything I sat on would be settled and I said when I got to be a lawyer I intended to "quash" all my cases (not let them come to trial you know) and Ida seemed to think I would be equal to it. I weigh *220* pounds now, aint that dandy?

Mr Wever said he had a lot of fun with Mr McKeighan this Spring. He said he made up his mind to see Mr Brown and if he wasn't going to give me the school here that he would hold the directorship till July and persuade me to take the Spring term just to pay Mc for his hatefulness but he found out Mr Brown had given me the school so he waited till all the business was attended to then handed in his resignation recommending Sam McKeighan as the proper man for the place. Of course he had the fun of watching him *squirm* all through the meeting.

I didn't know it before but last winter that Mrs Bacon told in Avoca that I didn't know enough to teach school and someone asked Bert about it and he told them that I "knew enough to teach the smartest that *that* district could show up."

You see they seem to feel as though I had to take all this on their account although they were not to blame for it so they have stood by me through all of this and I have just begun to discover what lot they have done for me.

Say Mrs Wever thought she was telling me *news* when she said she was positive that Gertie had caused me about as much trouble as any one. I just said quietly that "I knew it" and when I looked up there was the queerest look on her face you ever saw and she said if I had just said a word to her she would have put a stop to it mighty quick.

Sunday after dinner Bert, Ida, Gertie, Lee and I walked over to Buckleys who are now living between Wevers and Tennant. Bert hadn't been feeling very well but thought the walk would do him good but he was worse by the time we got to Buckleys he laid down on the bed and when he got up to go out to look at the new pig pen his face was flushed and his eyes shone like glass and when he came in he took with a chill and wore Sam's coat and over coat home and then shivered.

You know that Carl who was at Wevers well they found out that he had hired to his brotherinlaw before he ever went to Wevers and *intended* to quit Wevers as soon as Spring work commenced—just worked them a little you know to get a months wages—well he quit so that left all the work for Bert and Sam B__[1] they put in 100 acres of corn last week in five days and have more than that much more to put in I dont see what on earth they will ever d[o] if Bert gets sick.

After Wevers went home I started [to] get ready to go on over to Shaffers and Frank didn't want me to go and Mildred set up a howl and said she wanted Bessie to stay and Martha wanted me to stay so I stayed there all night and this morning it was raining to beat the band. it let up a little at half after seven so I struck out as Sam has no rig of any sort I hoofed it through the mud *two miles* and got to Shaffers and got my clothes changed and back to school by school time.

It was so rainy that I didn't have much of a school today just ten pupils

Tonight Mr Shaffer went to Tennant and he brought me a letter from the Co. Supt. saying that the T'w'p examination for Shelby Twp would be held at No. 5 May 17 and inclosing a *special* letter from the Supt. saying that He wanted me to hold the examination for my pupils at our school and send him the papers. he inclosed the questions. Now I think *that* shows that he has some confidence in me even if there has been a heap of trouble. (You know Wevers and he are good friends).

Did I tell you that when I was in Harlan I got the stuff for the pennant for our school and left it for Aunt Jennie to do in tufted work TENNANT

I am to go down to No 5 the evening of the 17th to help in the arrangement for the picnic.

Yes I'll give Uncle S__ a try. whats his address? Momence?

So you didn't know my throat ever bothered me? well I declare have you forgotten how it used to itch till it nearly drove me crazy? but thats about all it bothered. Thats enough though

Much obliged for those stamps. What handkerchiefs? I dont catch on. What do you call the *new* sorrel?

When you wash *this week* wash *next week* along with. Tell Robert that Mabel or "Billy Shaffer" as he is pleased to call her will have caniptions if he doesn't write next time. I would be much obliged to Fuller if he would send me Lewis Hansens letter to read as I could get an idea of Dakota—would return at once.

Erle Hamler (my mischief) wants the boys to subscribe for "The American Boy" it is a real good boys paper, excelent in a literary way it comes once a month and costs $1 a year. Its just fine and the boys would go wild over it and I believe its what Fuller needs. I could send you a paper so you could see what it is like if you wish and would send it back.

Sam Buckley has taken the agency for a picture enlarging outfit and he wants me to give him an order to start with—he said he would have papa's picture enlarged for me at cost if I would give him the first order it would cost me $3 or $3.50 for what would cost $5.00 around here. I would be glad to if you say the word.

Well it is late so I will stop or you will have to pay postage so no more at present

Yours as ever

Bess.

Will be going some all of this week so no telling when you will hear from me again.

1. Sam Buckley.

. . . .

MAY 20, 1906 TENNANT, IOWA

To Mrs. E. O. Corey, Elmdale

Dear Mamma,—Recovered from the last dose yet? If you have I'll give you another.

I dont know whether I told you in my last letter that I had received a letter from the Co. Supt. in which was a notice of a teachers meeting at No 5 May 17 at 7:30 P.M. to make arrangements for the School Picnic. well I made up my mind right away that I could not go way down there that time of night. That evening Perle Savage who teaches No 5 called me up to see if I was coming down, for as she boards at home, in Shelby, she did not wish to stay out there till that time of night unless there was sure to be others there. well later in the evening I called her up and suggested that if we could not all make connections Thursday evening perhaps we could all meet on Saturday and she thought that would be alright. Wednesday evening I went up to Hallorans and stayed all night and had a pleasant time—received your letter.

Thursday I started to give the exam's to three of my pupils—don't think any of them will pass—discovered when it was to late that they knew nothing of square root, cube root and longitud and time—had always skipped that, so they say. Of course they blame all of their former teachers but thank goodness they think I did all that I could for them and if they had not been quite so stubbern they would have learned a good deal more than they have.

Thursday evening when I got home I found that Perle Savage had called up the night before while I was gone to say that they were not going to have the picnic as none of the teachers wanted it—well I called up Ruth Myers to see how she was getting on with the exam and found that the same word had been sent to Miss Morris, their teacher, and they were all much dissapointed so Friday Morning I went down to see Mr Brown and he said to invite the neighboring schools. that is No 1, No 3 and Pioneer to join us and have our picnic in the Tennant grove so we will have it in the Tennant Grove June 1 but what I don't like is that it throws the responsibility onto me—and its a big chunk of responsibility too to run a picnic in a place like this I will be so busy these next few weeks that you need expect no letters from me.

Saturday forenoon I made me *ten new* collars—all dandys—in the afternoon we went up to Tennant as it was the grand opening of the new store—yes there are two general stores in Tennant now. I phoned to Aunt Jennie and she said she would get the pennant and badges to me by the last of this week.

Say what do you think? Mrs McK told the teacher that Mrs Wever wasn't going to let Gertie take the T'w'p exam because she didn't have time to review up so the teacher didn't send Gertie any word about the exam and Gertie has lost her last chance.

Shaffers were going over to Will's today and I wanted to stay at home and lay around and read and sleep but they had all planned so much on my going and were so dissapointed when I asked to be excused—why they scolded and coaxed and fineally said they would all stay at home if I did so I got ready and went—had a good time and didn't come home till after supper.

Yes I aught to have between fifty and sixty dollars when I get through here but I had intended to pay up that last years insuernce but suppose I can let that go—if I spend all that on my trip I wont have any for Summer School and I wanted to pay myself back that six dollars you gave me last Spring and say could you use some of my old waists and new ones too? that old brown one and blue one are too worn out for me and I'm getting so fat that several of my other waists, my new "yaller buff" one included, have got so they fit just horrid—its no go I've got to get rid of them and if you can make them over a little or use them to advantage so much the better.

Mrs Shaffer and I were both in the Tennant Bank that day she 'phoned—we just wanted to see if we could and how well we could hear. Your just right shes a good one.

Did you have to set the south pasture fence in as you thought you would? Hows the garden and crops? What are you going to name the colt?

Yes I'd give a "lick" at my piece of candy to be home long enough to can 60 qts of pieplant.

I'm sorry about Mrs Wheeler—don't forget to tell me how she is getting along when you write.

I though[t] I told you that I had no pattern for Ethels dress—just take any old pattern of hers and cut it over to suit her measure and do the rest by guess—thats the way I did.

I most forgot to tell you that I had the pleasure of meeting Ray Morris who is the Edwin Armstrong of this neighborhood he is less than a year older than I am. I like him dandy.

There is just one more month of School and with the picnic the last day decoration day and my sewing I have about three times as much as I can do and seem to feel so tired already.

I seem to stand a good show of getting every one satisfied before school lets out and I think most all of them will like me—I hope to remind my enemies of a few lines of a piece—

The harder your thrown

The higher you bounce

Be proud of your blackened eye

It isn't the fact that your licked that counts

But how did you fight and *why*?

The more they say against me the more friends I seem to have so perhaps they will give it up as a bad job.

Well I must close and retire for the clock has stopped though it was after nine when I started.

Mabel wrote to Robert this evening but I think Ethel aught to answer the letter Edward Miller wrote her last fall.

Yours as ever—Bess.

. . . .

MAY 27, 1906 TENNANT, IOWA

To Mrs. E. O. Corey, Elmdale

Dear Mamma,—How you vas? We're so cold we are like the dutch-man "shust about so leaf live as die."

I've about made up my mind that there is something or other wrong down there or I wouldnt have felt so homesick and lonesome these last few days.

I walked up to Tennant or rather I "went up town" Friday evening to meet the other teachers and make "arrangements" for the picnic. Miss Morris didn't get there and that left it to Miss Stewart Miss

McFarland and myself There was but one "arrangement" made and that was for me to see to getting the grove cleaned, getting some one to fix seats, getting the use of the church organ and getting some one to move it for us, and see to other small details In fact I—the youngest of the four—have the responcibility of every thing and will get, as I told Ida Wever, *some* of the praise *most* of the work and *all* of the cussing.

I wouldn't mind the work if some one else had the responcibility but as the picnic is in our grove its up to me so I will have to do my best and take what I get.

Saturday I scrubbed my head and had my hair dry before nine oclock—when my hair is brushed back the ends just touch the top of my belt I made my black sateen waist—got it all done and its fine I made it with a yoke and full front so it wont get too small. I got a new tie and belt like the scrap of ribbon enclosed to wear with it so you see it wont look so sober.

One of the windows in my spacious apartment fits very tightly and it generaly takes two hands and all ones strength to raise it but last night some how I let it slip down and catch one finger. You bet your Sunday shirt I got it up pretty quick with one hand that time. I thought my finger was broken but it was just crushed and it looks pretty bum yet.

Slept most of this forenoon and we all went to church in Tennant this afternoon—If Olney had been at Sunday School he would have given Mr Hamler an argument. I'll admit I was shocked to find that some people believe that God can't do much if men dont help him. Why if I didn't think that God was ever present and all powerful and was protecting me I'd get out of this neighborhood the quickest way and what is more I dont know where on earth I'd go to.

I was talking to Aunt Jennie over the phone—if she don't quit working so hard she will tear some of her clothes some of these days

I most forgot to tell you that I saw Ida, Gertie and Bert at Church— Bert has recovered from his "ager shills" but he and Ida are both looking thin.

Say is the new sorrel a gentleman or lady and whats *its* name

We are all going to Shelby Decoration Day but I wish I was going to be home just think I've only had a chance to visit papas grave just once and I'll not be home for a long long time yet.

Aunt Jennie has got a notion from something I said that I'm going somewhere as soon as my school is out. I wish I knew what to tell her cause I'm afraid her feet will begin to sweat pretty soon if something dont happen.

Booooo how cold it is!!! if you find any of my teeth or collar buttens you'll know how to account for them

I suppose Olney will be delighted to hear that Uncle Jim's health is much improved. I wonder why Grandma don't answer that letter I wrote her so long ago but then I suppose she hears all she wants to of me from you and Aunt Jennie. Aunt Jennie said something about her coming up is she? Tell her I'd be glad to hear from her any time.

I must go to roost—its awful late Come to the picnic June lst

Yours as Ever

Elisabeth F Corey

[Enclosure: a sample of ribbed fabric, deep rose in color]

. . . .

JUNE 3, 1906 TENNANT, IOWA

To Mrs. E. O. Corey, Elmdale

Dear Mamma,—It seems so *very* long since I got a letter from you but I suppose you are all very busy I know every one around here seems to be and I know I am.

Last Tuesday it rained so that only five or six of the pupils nearest could get to school—Wednesday was Decoration Day so we had no school—I went to Shelby with Shaffers—had a fine time—we went down early in the morning returning at about six in the evening. Ida Gertie and Brother Bert were there and I was with them about all day—had peanuts, candy, ice-cream, dinner at the hall and all the rest of it and it didn't cost *me* a cent. There were a great many there that I knew and you remember my telling you of a Mr George Slaughter—a widower who sat up at Tattmans the same night I was there well I saw him and spoke to him soon after we entered the cemetary—shortly after that we went up near the gate where the band was playing and pretty soon I noticed him talking to a gentleman standing near us but thought nothing of it. We went down town and took dinner at the Hall and when we came out there was Mr Slaughter talking to someone just out side the door but I didn't think nothing of that either, but, when the whole after noon, no matter where we went I couldn't glance across the street without seeing Mr Slaughter talking to a man just opposite I began to think it was strange for it wasn't two or three times it was more than a dozen times. We went into Ream's Store before starting home and when I came out I passed Mr Slaughter at the door and a mile or so out of town I ask who that was just ahead of us and just then the man turned around and to be sure it was Mr Slaughter. Now do you suppose all of that happened by accident or did some of it happen on purpose?

Thursday most of the pupils were at school and we did a good deal of practiceing. Friday morning early Mr Brown phoned up that he was going to Shelby and so could not help with the seats at the picnic so I had to get ready and go up early to see about things—I went to see the drayman who stopped in the middle of unloading a car of lumber and hauled two loads of plank for seats—then I went to see Mr Moury and Mr Bartholomew who quit their painting, which they wished to finish by noon, and came and put up the seats and stage for me by that time most of my pupils were there and the other schools had commenced to come and it seemed that "Miss Corey" was wanted every where at once. We Schoolma'ams went up town and got the material for lemonade and while we were makeing it the mammas in the crowd put the dinner on and then I waited rather, helped wait on table till every one was threw eating then Miss Stewart, Miss McFarland, Bessie Grauel and I sat down—I don't know how much we ate. After dinner we began to think about getting the organ over—Ida and I started to hitch up a team but made up our minds we couldnt get it in the wagon so Elmer Myers, Miss McFarland, Bess Grauel, Ida and I went over to the church—Miss McF— took the organ stool the rest of us took the organ and we carried it over to the grove while the crowd stood with mouths open far enough to swallow us all. We then made out our program, rallied the crowd and commenced. They tried to put reading the program on to me too but I wouldn't stand for that with all the extras to see to so Miss McF— who had nothing else to do agreed to read it. I had plenty to see to just to manage part of the crowd. Anna Stewart was down from Harlan but Mr Luxford did not put in appearance to present Ruth Myers her Diploma Ruth was one of my pupils last fall and winter and the only one who passed. The crowd, numbering about one hundred and fifty people, broke up about five oclock all reporting a fine program and good time. I reached home about half after six—tired? well I guess!!!

If you don't want the badge enclosed you can send it to Grandma but I thought perhaps you might like to keep it as it is the one your little girl wore at the picnic June 1.

Yesterday forenoon I cut out a waist and slept the rest of the time—in the afternoon I made my waist, didn't get it finished cause I made one sleve wrong and just as I got it ripped out Mabel came in with your card which almost frightened me to death—we could not imagine what you meant by "a most hopeless case right here." I went up town and the elevator man called you folks up and I talked to Olney didn't get much satisfaction only that you were all well so I've about made up my mind that something has hapened to Valerie or money matters are off or I dont know just what but I am waiting your explaination with all the patience I can muster

Mr Shaffers father is pretty bad off so they went to Shelby today—wanted me to go along but I begged of and as there is no good time piece here I have almost lost track of time. I called up centeral and got the time at half after one then laid down here on the floor to finish going over the lesson & write to you so it must be pretty late by this time.

If you can, plan on having one of the boys come up to Shaffers after me June 17th I'm coming home for one night any way

Yours as Ever—Bess.

[At top of first page:] Have ordered two new skirts one gray one brown the two will cost nine or ten dollars.

Harlan

After her school dismissed for the year, Bess came home to the farm for a week before leaving again for Harlan, where she had arranged to board at the home of her aunt, Jennie Corey Dunlavy (also a teacher), while attending the 1906 Summer School. Jennie and her husband, James D. Dunlavy, "J. D.," who had a few years before been a superintendent of schools for the county, had recently moved into Harlan from the hamlet of Corley. The Dunlavy home was apparently brand new and had more than one spare room, for Bess mentions in her first letter that she is the "only boarder . . . as yet." Throughout the letters in this section, Bess's uneasy relationship with her uncle, and less often, her aunt, is evident. The Dunlavys had no children.

Bess's paternal aunts (l-r) Rachel, Mattie, Jennie, and Mary Corey. Jennie Corey Dunlavy provided a home for Bess during the summer of 1906 while she attended summer school.

JUNE 26, 1906 HARLAN, IOWA

To Mrs. E. O. Corey, Elmdale

Dear Mamma,—How did Fuller get home? Was there any thing wrong down there between five and eight oclock Sunday evening?

I am the only boarder here as yet and so have been favored with the "east room." at first they said for me to leave my trunk in the store room for fear it would scratch up the floor of the east room. I didn't like that plenty cause it would be so unhandy to have to go through the hall to the store room every time I wanted any thing and beside *that*, just as sure as I was in undress uniform and wanted some article from my trunk to complete my toilet, for instance some article of wearing apparil, which might be unmentionable, "*J.D.*" would be sure to be investigating some thing or other in the store room and that would be so—well you know—well finealy they decided that I might put it in the closet cause if I got things scratched up there it wouldnt show much. I have a good bed and Aunt Jen told me where I could get one of the old comforts she used over the sofa down on the farm to put over the bed to keep the quilts clean and I may also put it on the floor if I like I also have a wash stand a dressing table and two sort of window seats with out any backs in fact they are boxes of book[s] covered and set crossways of the corners. they have promised me a rocking chair but it hasn't arrived yet and I cant bring it up alone with out a chance of scratching something so I have no chair as yet and at present am stretched at full length, front side down, beneath the one small window, with my twenty or more text and reference books with in reach. Tell the boys they need not begrudge me my good times, for they would laugh till you would have to set their ears back if they could see their weighty relative stepping cautiously from rug to rug avoiding walls and furniture as if they were so many edges of a needle book—you know the walls are so white and might get soiled.

Summer School opened yesterday with a much smaller attendance than last year. I like all of the instructors. Mr Asquith is just—oh I cant express it he is *so* nice. I had to go up town yesterday afternoon and that wasted quite a bit of time so after I had put three hours on a twenty five page Physics lesson and three more hours on a thirty page Algebra lesson my time was gone and I had to bluff it through on the rest. Mr Asquith asked me about a third of all the questions and

I answered them too and after class he spoke to me about a book of his and ask me if I had one like it and as I hadn't one he gave me his to read and said I could leave it on his desk when ever I got through with it. What makes folks so good to me? I suppose its because they dont know me. I take Physics, Economics and Didactics under Mr Asquith and Algebra Civics Music and History under Mr Peterson and am going to try and get time to study some of the other branches too.

Yesterday when I was up town I went up to Stod Wick's office with his sister Grace. Grace was trying to decide whether to attend Summer School or not—I said I thought she better and Stodd said he thought so too and when she asked why he said a girl like her aught to have something on her mind she said she did have *something* on her mind & he said "yes that big hair ribbon for instance" but that wasn't just what she aught to have on her mind. I think thats the way with lots of them now days.

Sunday evening Aunt Jen told me to go to the cupboard and get what I wanted to eat. yesterday we had dinner at ten minutes to one and to day at five minutes to one

My but its after three and I must get to work for I would rather work all day and night to than have Mr Asquith ask me a question that I couldn't answer.

so long

Bess.

P.S. I finished my letter but when I rolled over I thought of some more—Emmet Naugle and family have been visiting Mrs J O Corey and family of Atlantic Did you *get that*? And F B Corey and family have *moved* to Atlantic Did you *catch that*? Mr Naugle went down and hunted Frank up and Frank came up and took dinner with them. Hear *that*? Wireless telegraphy is a mighty fine thing.

· ·

JULY 3, 1906 HARLAN, IOWA

To Mrs. E. O. Corey, Elmdale

Dear Mamma,—I am just home from school and will endeavor to write you a record of my goodness badness & indifferance.

It is getting on towards one oclock and we havent had dinner yet but will have before I get this finished as Aunt Jennie has quit canning cherries and has started dinner for I can hear her pounding steak. The earliest we've had dinner yet was ten minutes to one the latest—well some hour or two later. Have got my self a cold lunch about five different evenings to save Aunt Jennie from getting hot supper but I wouldn't get a lunch even if my Uncle could prevent it. You just aught to hear some of these ladies talk!!! Its something like this

1st—Oh you just aught to see my boarder! She's so nice!

2nd—My boarder is the nicest little girl—no bother at all!

3rd—My boarder is the sweetest little girl you ever saw and dresses so pretty!!

4th—My boarder is absolutely no trouble at all—so easy to cook for!

Aunt Jennie—My boarder is so easy to cook for—why I can put her off with out any meals at all if I wish and its all right.

Yes I am Aunt Jennies "*boarder*" I received Ida's letter and will enclose it as it may interest you and I have answered it.

1:30 dinner over.

Last week Mr Asquith asked us all to hand in slips of paper with our names written on them and we did. He put them in a book and loaned me the book. a day or two later he had us hand in our names again and was going on at a great rate about having lost them out of his pocket. I told him afterward about finding them in the book and we had quite a laugh over it.

My room only has one window and Aunt Jennie was always saying to leave my door open as it would make it cooler well Thursday afternoon I took a nap after studying some time and that evening Uncle Jim told Mr Morril that I slept about three hours every afternoon so made up my mind I better keep my door shut and also *locked* even if I did roast.

Friday afternoon I took a bath in the bathtub. its just fine.

Saturday morning I went up town to get some things I wanted and some things Aunt Jen wanted and in the after noon I started Ethels dress. It was most all guess work as I didn't even have an old pattern to go by & I'm very anxious to know how much changeing will have to be done to make it fit. I had thought it was going to be pretty but before it was finished I almost hated to think of sending it. Uncle Jim's nose went up a degree farther and he made some remark about "apron stuff" and later on ask if I was making me a wrapper. Aunt Jennie asked why I gathered it on the sholder and if I was going to put insertion on the skirt and if I wasnt going to trim the goods from beneath the insertion.

Sunday Taylor Jacksons were here and yesterday after dinner I finished Ethels dress—didn't get it finished in time for the three o'clock train so called Sarah up to see if she was going down town she said she was going in the evening and for me to come up and go along. she said she would call up later and tell me when she would be ready to start. I went up stairs and tried to study but my head seemed to ache frightfully so I went to sleep. after a while Sarah called up and Uncle Jim answered the phone and told her that I had gone up town and so Aunt Jen supposed I had and didn't know the differance till supper time and then she told me what Uncle Jim had done so I went and called Sarah and she asked me when I got home—well we got things straightened out and I was to be up in half an hour. Supper was not ready yet and Uncle Jim roasted me for sleeping in the day time and studying at night and burning coal oil that cost them money. As I hadn't been studying *late* and wasn't feeling well I told Aunt Jen if I used more oil than most folks I would pay for it as an extra but *would* study when I pleased and as long as I pleased she said not to pay any atention to him but to use as much oil as I wished. I went up to Sarahs it was past time and Sarah had gone but would meet me at Fosters so I went to Fosters they had just closed—I stopped at Nielsons for those pins he fixed and by the time I got down to the Post Office it was past eight and the Office was closed so I didn't get to mail Ethels dress & missed the last chance of her getting it by the fourth. As I was comming home I saw Lida Smith standing on the porch and as I knew her mother was gone and she was alone I stopped awhile and did not get back to Dunlavys till half after nine. Dunlavys havent their new walks in yet but have the old ones torn up and as it has rained every day or night since I came up here it keeps this clay in a real nice shape for a block here making it an impossility to wear low shoes and as I had on long skirts last evening and my hands full of course it took a notion to shower while I was down town consequently my skirts are in a frightful shape and my new under skirt is ruined for ever and ever so much for a handy boarding place.

At dinner time Aunt Jennie was telling me something and Uncle

Jim roasted her proper. he told her that she knew very well that what she said went right up town and was talked about all over town. you bet that fetched my English up and before I went up stairs I said that I might have to take his remarks and mean insinuations for relations sake but I would never send a friend of mine here to board and I wont either. I half expect to get orders to move when I go down stairs but there are plenty of other boarding places if I do. I would hate to go on Aunt Jen's account for she has treated me pretty well and the meals suit me all right as I get plenty to eat and the time is immaterial to me. It did bother me Sunday evening when Aunt Jen sent me to the cupboard to get a lunch and Uncle Jim said he shouldnt think I would want any supper after eating so much dinner & ended by saying that I wasn't to eat any of that cold pork steak as there was enough there for breakfast. He also insinuates that I dont earn the good grades I get—now I speak of it we had a History test Friday and I got a good grade which pleased me very much as our grades are brought up for or against us in final exams. Will enclose my test paper so you can see I earned what I got.

I wonder what you folks are going to do tomorrow I will either study or move

Well I must close for now. will try to write more next time.

Yours With Love

Bess.

[No Enclosures]

* *

JULY 8, 1906 HARLAN, IOWA

To Mrs. E. O. Corey, Elmdale

Dear Mamma,—I wonder what you are all doing. This is the 8*th* and I wrote you on the third but it seems an age ago. How did Paulie celebrate his birthday? I wish I was there to help him a little while.

After I finished that last letter to you I went down and called up Sarah and as she was going down town and so was I, we decided to go together so I went up to Sarahs. Before we got started Lida Smith called up from down town and wanted us to meet her at a certain corner so we did. There was a fortune teller at Kuhls Hotel for a week and Sarah and a lot of other girls had been down the night before and had their fortunes told and they all got so much fun out of it that Sarah wanted us to get ours told. I didn't want to at first but Lida was going so I went along and oh such a picnic. She told me all about the past and present and future. I don't believe in such things but got my moneys worth of fun out of it. she told me, among others things, that this spring while I was boarding away from home that a light complected girl just coming into her teens took two letters from my mail and gave them to a dark complected woman. they were just friendship letters but if I had expected to receive letters and did not for me to write to my friends and find out about it she said that dark woman had tried to make me trouble but had failed. I thought at once of Mrs Shaffer and Mabel and of the letters from Flora Koeppe and others that I wondered why I did not receive. she said I would be married and in a home of my own in six months and I stamped my foot and declared I *would not* and she declared I would & fineally said to wait and see and I told her I certainly would *wait*. she then undertook to describe the unfortunate gent and she did too. before she got through Sarah & Lida both recognized it as the exact description of Bert Wever why she even said he was just a little past twenty six years old and had a E. and a V. in his name. oh how those girls laughed! but my turn came and I more than got even with them.

I went home with Sarah and stayed all night. she called up Dunlavys to tell them I was going to stay and Uncle Jim said he was "Glad of it." The next morning we went down town to see the parade and met the Wever young folks on the corner—Bert was swelled up like fifty cents in a new suit and hat. I never saw him look so nice. I vonder vy I vonder vy While we were standing there watching the sights George Stewart came up and I said something to him and he steped to my side in his usual easy way and bent his head to hear what I had to say and what do you think? Bert's eyes turned from brown to green in an instant and he turned right to Gertie and said something to her and held her parasol for her.

I was with Wevers all day and we persuaded Bert to go down and have his fortune told. We went along but he wouldn't let us listen to it. When Bert came out Gertie ask him how many times he was going to get married and he said seven or eight. the fortune teller laughed and said we knew better than that and when Bert turned she winked at me so when they started to go out I steped back and asked her what she meant and she said he was the man that I would marry but for heaven sake not to tell. Isn't that funny? I just felt like hitting every one I saw for a while.

Oh you don't need to worry—there is no danger really and fortune teller's talk is all foolishness.

There were dozens of people here the fourth that I knew.

It rained here quite hard in the afternoon but we were in the Court House and did not get wet Wevers went home about five and left me with Lida Smith. we soon found the Stewart crowd and were with them till we went home for supper. After supper I went down to Smiths. Lida and I went down to the post office and then went down to see the fire works and I didn't get home till late. I didn't spend a single cent but had peanuts candy fruit and chopped suie the latest thing in the shape of ice cream it is figs and hickory nut meats chopped up and mixed in the cream and is just fine though very rich. I had more than I could eat and politely refused one treat

The next day I went to school as usual but every one was sleepy and no one seemed to know any thing. I cut the last few recitations and came home—too much confectionary I am ashamed to say.

Yesterday I was up to Stewarts from seven oclock in the morning till after supper. Sarah is helping me make my white dress of Indian head linen a kind of heavy white goods. It is just a shirt waist suit but will be very pretty. I wish I had a piece here to send you.

Sarah had the impudance to ask if it was my weding dress and then nearly had jiminy fits over the way I took it.

Sarah thinks Bert is awful nice and you know she got acquainted with Ida at the sewing school last summer. well she asked me if I supposed Bert and Ida would come up some Sunday if she ask them and if they did if I wouldn't come up too. I said I would. She wants me to go down to Wevers with her and George some Sunday. But I dont know about that I guess Gertie wants Bert worse than I do and I will stay clear away and let her have him.

Uncle Jim wont speake to me any more but complains to Aunt Jen constantly. He kept his eye [on] me all day the fourth—I didn't make a move that he didn't see I guess. Aunt Jennie never went down town at all the fourth.

Mr. G W Wever went to Missouri July 3rd dont know when he will return.

When did Mrs Sorensen go back east?

My but I am at it hard these days! In trying for a first grade certfi-cate I may fail to get even a second grade but Im trying and—

As to the future tis not ours to say

What shall be whether Yay or nay.

Well it is ten oclock and I must retire as I have a hard week before me.

I would like to have a letter from you but suppose you are very busy.

Uncle Franks children visit grandma nearly every day but the whole family went to Shenandoah for the fourth—"excursion rates I presume"

Grandma had received a "letter from Maggie" but supposed I had been told all the news so would not repeat it.

Aunt Jennie offered me Aunt Rates last letter to read but I didn't read it. I offered her your letter to read and she read it to but did not remind me that I left out one page.

Yours with Love

Bess *Corey*

. . . .

JULY 15, 1906 HARLAN, IOWA

To Mrs. E. O. Corey, Elmdale

Dear Mamma,—Your letter was recived the middle of the week but I did not feel equal to giving it to Aunt Jennie to read.

No I dont think Uncle Jim delayed or opened any of my mail but he always managed to dodge around the corners and get to the post office first and if there was any mail for me he knew all about it befor I did and I got a notion that something was wrong and so went down July 5*th* and told them that in the future to hold my mail till I called for it.

Uncle Jim treats me pretty well now but roasts Aunt Jennie for letting me use the bath tub and she just says that's what its for and to use it as often as I wish. Oh I want to tell you a good one on him. I noticed that he didn't eat so much at meal time and he soon began to go on about people eating so much and Aunt Jen said "Just you hush up. Youd eat a lot more if you hadn't been to the cupboard stuffing all the forenoon." He declared he hadn't and she said he lied.

I don't want to write to James Boland but if you would go around that way some time when you are going to Walnut and find out if he has a teacher engaged and if not speak for me I will be much obliged to you and if it looks good to you I'll write to him later.

Dont sweat your feet thinking about those *seventeen* girls getting thir certificates, they will be a lucky crowd if they *all* do.

Dont expect to much of me mamma. there was only one other girl in the class who has not taken these branches before and that other girl has given up First Grade. The Co Supt. thinks I am working against odds and so do I and if I do better than make a flat failure it will be that much better than I expect. But I'm still trying

Mr Asquith loaned me another book Friday and one of the girls got ahold of it and found his name in it and I tell you they roasted me good and proper for having a "stand in" with one of the instructors. Friday afternoon I went down to the schoohouse to hear Mr Peterson explain some problems to the girls and vat you tink? Mr Peterson made me a presant of an answer book. My!!! those girls will have jiminie fits now.

I seem to have had the leg ache awful yesterday and this morning—havent been up town or to church but guess I will be able to go to school tomorrow as I feel first rate tonight.

This morning after Aunt Jennie went to Sunday School I went down stairs and Uncle Jim had gone for a walk out in the country so I called up Wevers and—just my onery luck—the folks was away, the girls down to the pasture and no one there but Bert so we had quite a nice little talk—Berts folks gone and my folks gone and no one to hear but the neighbors. He recovered from the effects of the fourth,— has been very busy the past week has put up *two* (2) loads of hay— his father returned from Missouri and has purchased land in Dent County which is the second county north of Howell where you were. They are going to move in the fall or winter. Bert said he would tell Ida to call me up when she got back but she hasn't so I rather expect that horrid man *forgot* it. Guess he was afraid to tell for fear Gertie would scold him.

So you ate so many fire crackers that you had the stomach ache the next day. too bad!! Fire crackers must be bad medicine, George[1] and I think *green apples* are *bad enough*.

I've found out where Uncle Jim keeps that beer that he says the preacher gave him and its awful good.

So Paul tried on Ethels dress and Ethel made him a birthday for his cake. I'm glad it fit him so well.

I'm going to send Paul a Postal Card one of these days would like to be a mouse and hear what he says. Tell him I said if he wasn't a better boy I'm going to send that Batty sherif down after him and have him brought up here where the judge sets on Court plaster and the Jury bring in a verticl stick and rope and bind him over to the Grand Jury and they will take him to the pen where he will have to wash his feet sixteen times and comb his hair with a tooth pick and then if he aint good they will give him to Uncle Jim. so will you be good now?

Chautauqua will commence Saturday August 4*th*. If one of the boys come up I think we can get season tickets for *two* of us for three dollars and then if you and one of the other boys drive up the next Thursday morning us two could get our tickets transfered to you two and we could drive home Thursday evening and you take it in Thurs Friday Sat and Sunday that would be fair all around and I would have to miss just one day of Institute and you could attend the Episcopal Church Sunday morning and if it was to far from here to the Chautauqua grounds you could stay with Sarah and go down after dinner and take a lunch like many others do and not come back till after it is over in the evening. It will be a good change for you and you could make it quite a rest by doing that way.

Well it is getting on twords eleven pretty fast and I must get up tomorrow morning and study some more so will close hoping to hear from you soon I am

Yours—Bess.

1. George Stewart, according to family tradition, was Bess's only serious beau during her schoolteaching years in Iowa.

· ·

JULY 19, 1906 HARLAN, IOWA

To Mrs. E. O. Corey, Elmdale

Dear Mamma,—Well where are you at now? I'm in my favorite position, stret[c]hed front side down on a comfort on the floor in my room. I don't know what I'm writing you on Thursday for unless its because its my blue week.

I've been doing some wonders in school this week and hope to accomplish some more wonderful wonders befor next Saturday eve.

Tuesday evening Uncle Jim and I had another time like Mr Pingle makes for the teacher. Aunt Jennie kept saying it wasn't so and for me not to pay any attention to him but of course she couldn't make him stop and so I just sat and took it and never said a word but could hardly finish my supper and bawled my temper out after I went up stairs. Its all over now so I aught not have mentioned it.

Wednesday morning I wasn't hungry so asked to be excused from breakfast and when I started to school I told Aunt Jennie not to wait dinner for me as I did not know what time I would be back.

I intended to go up town after school but it looked so rainy and I had no rubbers or umberella so decided to go home but by the time I had gone three or four blocks it was raining. I was under a row of large trees so did not notice it much at first but when I got to Smiths corner it was just pouring down. there were no more trees to shelter and three more blocks to go so I just ran across to Smiths as Lida had asked me several times to take dinner and spend the afternoon with her.

After dinner I was taken with cramps and Lida put me to bed. I took a book along but did not study very much—got to sleep after a while and had quite a nap. About six oclock Lida and I got ready to go down town but didn't go till after supper. After we got through up town we went up to Stewarts and stayed a while—had lots of fun & brought my new dress home with me. Its just fine.

When I was coming up the street Uncle Jim called and said I might walk on the new side walk, so they have them in at last after I have ruined two pair of shoes—just a little matter of five or six hard earned dollars. I tell you what! when I come to foot up this summers bills, last summers expences will be clear in the shade. I've given up the suit case and in a week or two you will get a note something like the young man wrote his pa—

Roses are red, violets are blue

Please send ten dollars and I'll owe you.

so you better save up your pennies.

Mamma I'm the worstest little girl you've got. Why didn't you spank me oftener when I was under your jurisdiction? Today the history recitation wasn't going to amount to anything for me so I just cut it and came home. Well I went down to the Post Office first—walked down with Miss White and just as we were going the last block a gentleman who was walking behind us stepped up and asked me some question and walked down with us. He went and got his mail but I had to wait quite a while to get mine. Miss White lives north of the post office but I and this other gentleman live south and I wondered why he hurried out after getting his mail and did not wait for me. well he went back to the school house and went up and got his books and was going on across the school yard by the time I got to the school house. He soon discovered that *he was ahead* of me instead of *me being ahead* of him and he began to step around every lose brick or hit it with his umberella but I didn't really catch on that he was *waiting* for me till he had glanced back two or three times. Well just for orneryness, and because there were some ladies watching the preformance I dodged around the corner and went up the other street and was out of sight before he knew it. I dont know why I played him such a trick for he is one of the nicest men in town and has been very kind to me and I like him ever so much. It began to rain like sixty when I had gone about two blocks which made me almost wish he was holding the umberella for me but then its just as well he wasnt for he might have felt it his duty to carry it the rest of the way for me and then Aunt Jennie would have given me jiminie fits

We had a test in Civics today and mine was O.K. and I also got another good grade in Didactics we are to have a stemwinder of a test in History tomorrow including every thing from Columbus to Lincoln perhaps I wont have to take examination in all fourteen branches for they say that the branches we got above 90% in last year we dont have to take this year.

I can hear a little boy two blocks east of here calling "Here Max here Max" to his dog and it makes me think of Paulie.

Well I must change my duds and gather up my books and get to work so good by

Bess

P.S. Say ma I wish you would look through those papers in that black valice and find my reports of examination. they are three different cards about as large as postal cards and have my grades on them. It may take some time and I hate to bother you but if you could get them to me soon it would save me many hours of hard work.

E. F. C.

One of them might be in the sitting room book case.

JULY 24, 1906 HARLAN, IOWA

To Mrs. E. O. Corey, Elmdale

Dear Mamma,—Oh my goodness but the mostest things have happened since I wrote you last. I bet I'll make you pay two cents to get this letter.

Last Friday morning Miss Graves (Miss Reynolds cousin) was late and didn't get the problems written down in physics and late in the afternoon she phoned up to see if I had them and when she found I had, she said she would come up. Well she came up after supper and copied the problems and then we worked till about ten o'clock. I was going to go a ways with her and we started out but didn't get far for Miss Graves made a misstep and fell from the walk to the pavement and almost broke her ankle but escaped with just a terrible sprain and broken ligaments. I called Uncle Jim to phone for the buss but Mr Merril who was talking to Uncle Jim on the porch said it was too near train time for the buss to come and insisted on going for his horse and buggy. By the time he had caught, harnessed and hitched up the horse, it was half after ten. I went along & we almost carried Edith into the house. They had the doctor come up and strap it and it is getting on as well as can be expected but I have been sending down the assignments of the lessons for her so she could keep up with the work as she was worrying so about not going to school and feared she would fail to get first grade.

Aunt Jennie finished the south room Friday evening. and I took such a liking to it that I asked to be allowed to move in right away instead of waiting till someone else came first. Aunt Jennie was very glad to have me move so I did and she went right to work fixing up the east room so it would be all fine and dandy if any one came.

After I moved and got my things straightened around I took a bath and dressed for dinner. After dinner Sarah called up to say that she could not sew in the afternoon so I did not go up. Stayed at home and meant to study but put in most of my time tending my headache.

Sunday morning Aunt Jennie went to Sunday School and stayed to church and Uncle Jim went to church and I stayed at home and studied my own Sunday School Lesson. Mr Book Store Miller was here to dinner and in the afternoon I studied. I called Sarah up to see if she was going to church and she wasn't as she had just returned from a picnic out at Frank Stoleys. Frank Stoley is brother to Valeries Fred. and by the way this Clara Stoley who attends Summer School is a sister of Valeries Fred. George answered the phone but didn't know who I was and so I had him call Sarah and when he found it was me he said it was a good thing for me he didn't know who I was. Joe put in and said for me to come up that he wanted to see me and I said for him to come down and Sarah said she didn't dare to let him for fear my "fortune" would come true. I told her it was to late and Joe said better late than never. Sarah said she would come along and fan him and I said for goodness sake to bring some one along to fan me. When Sarah got ready to hang up Joe said good bye and I said "good bye I hope it aint for long." I just thought if he wanted to act the fool I would keep even.

I almost forgot to tell you that Friday noon when I was coming home that Ida and Mrs Wever overtook me and we stopped and talked for about twenty minutes I believe. They told me about the new home in Missouri and began planning right away for me to come down and visit them when they get settled but those ornery girls insinuate that in reality Wevers plan to take me along. The new home is on a mountain side and has a big house and ten acres of orchard and they are about a mile from the school and the farm that Sam Buckley talks of buying is just half a mile from school. I'm almost dying to know what Bert is going to do but wouldn't ask for the world. Ida is going to get up during Chautauqua so perhaps we will get in some visit then.

Yesterday after dinner we heard the door bell and Aunt Jennie had her mout[h] chuck full of gum and couldn't find any place to put it so I had to go to the door, and there was that handsome Mr Nealen who attended Institute last year. he had come to engage board for the next three weeks and his sister will be here by the middle of next week.

I spent yesterday afternoon with Sarah and stayed to supper I knew I was about all in this summer but didn't suppose that any one else noticed it but Sarah says I look so *awful tired all* the time and wants me to take a week off after Institute and rest up she says for me to come and stay with her, she says my board wont cost me any thing and I can sleep half the time or all the time if I want to. I have half a notion to take a week off and not think once about any of the worryments of life and just rest and get ready for school in the fall. I could run down to Tennant and spend a day or two with Ida you know

I promised her I would spend Aug 15th or the Sunday following with her if possible.

Say what do you think? Dunlavys have got so when any one phones up for me they insist on knowing who it is before they call me and it makes some folks kind of mad. Smiths are going to have a phone put in this week and Lida *vows* she will *never* tell them who she is.

Mr Nealon is *"just lovely."* we have gotten pretty well acquainted already and have begun to lend each other books and say I was almost mad yesterday cause just as soon as he was out of hearing Aunt Jennie gave me to understand that I must *behave myself while he was here.* I tell you what—such things as that just stir up all the devil in my make up.

One evening last week a young fellow and I were talking and I guess he thought he would show the other girls how smart he was and he said when he got ahold of any thing he held on to it and he caught my hand and when I tried to jurk away he put his arm around me, and may be you don't think something happened. I gave him a terrible slap and as he dodged he caught it the side of his head. I guess it must of hurt for he told the other girls th[at] he thought he was getting bawled and I told him *he would mighty quick* if he ever put his arm around me again.

Say have you found those reports of examination yet? I'm so anxious to get them I can hardly wait.

So you have been having some wet down there have you? Well I don't appreciate the wet like I did before the pavement was put in. Im afraid Mr Lanas¹ grade wont make the farm worth more than $100 per acre at that rate.

Do you find any advantage in making soap the new way?

Paul is something like Rob used to be isn't he? chuck full of the Old Nick. We wanted to come down after berries but couldn't either of us come alone and there wasn't room for all three and we couldn't leave Uncle Jim alone you know

You aren't going to let Olney have two weeks off for Chautauqua and not let Rob and Fuller have a single day are you?

I'm glad you are getting along so well. Please keep close track of that fruit till after you divide up with me.

Why I wish I had a school ingaged for next year so it would be off my mind.

My head aches so I can hardly see so will close Oh say I got 90% in this last history test and about that in civics test

As ever Yours

Bess,

1. According to Paul Corey, the Corey family often borrowed money from a Mr. Lana, who may have been someone Mr. Corey knew politically.

Irwin

SHELBY COUNTY, IOWA

JANUARY 1908 TO JUNE 1908

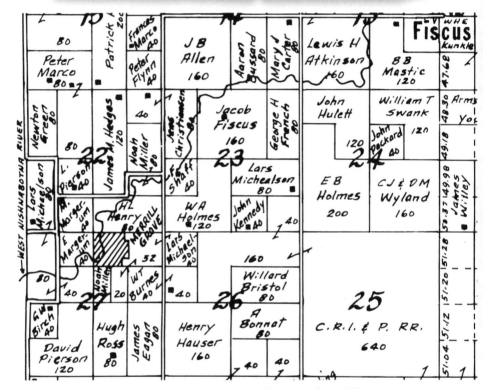

1884 plat map of Shelby County, showing the location of Merrill's Grove (straddling sections 22 and 27), where Bess probably taught school while living in Irwin. The town no longer exists, although there is a small cemetery near the old town site.

Bess appears to have lived at home and taught in her own township during the 1906–1907 school year and maybe even up until Christmas of the following year, since the next set of letters doesn't begin until January 1908. She may have taught at School #9, just a stone's throw from Corey Farm, a supposition supported by her great interest, in

The Martin Scott family of Merrill's Grove. (l-r), Martin Scott, Garnett Scott, and Anna Peterson Scott. Courtesy of Bernadine Gaer of Harlan, Iowa.

the following set of letters, in who is teaching at that school and how things are going there.

As 1908 opened, Bess had begun teaching near Irwin, Iowa, perhaps in Merrill's Grove, an area populated mostly by Danish families. Bess boarded with a family having the last name of Scott. Phil Gerber states that it was the Martin Scotts, and indeed the 1905 state census shows a Martin and Anna Scott living in the nearby hamlet of Kirkman, but they have no children. The names Bess mentions most in her letters: Petra (who is a dwarf, hence Bess's references to a "Lilliputian"), Sorine, Soren, and Millie Scott, may indicate she stayed with the Soren Scott family, listed in 1905 under the names Sorren, Johanna, Petrea, Sorine, and Milly *Skyt*. Martin was likely the twenty-one-year-old son of this Soren, as the 1900 federal census lists the children of Soren and his wife Hannah as Martin (16), Petrea (12), Serena (11), and Millie (8).

The Soren Scott family of Merrill's Grove. Back (l-r) Millie, Serena, Martin; front (l-r) Johanna, Petra, Soren. Courtesy of Bernadine Gaer of Harlan, Iowa.

JANUARY [16], 1908 IRWIN, IOWA

To Mrs. E. O. Corey

Dear Folks,—Have tried to reach you by phone for ever so long but it doesn't seem to do any good for when I do get you you can't hear me though I can hear you all right.

Am getting along alright but its just rush rush rush—so much going on and Scotts don't like to have me stay here alone. To begin at the beginning the evening I got here we had company and Mr & Mrs were away—I suppose Olney told you that—Then the next evening we were all over to Soren Scotts to a big Supper—The next evening we sat up and watched the old year out and the new year in and the old year made a lot of racket going out too—The next day was Gordens birthday and there were a *few* here to eat New Years dinner or supper which you may wish to call it and about midnight I guess it was we had ice cream & cake The next evening we had cake and coffee at Rev Jensens and were invited to a big dinner at Larsens for the next evening—of course we went and had a fine time the next day I had neuraliga of the head all day so I didn't do much but in the evening I helped Myrtle scrub her hair. Sunday we went to Church in the forenoon and Myrtle and Petra went to String Town. Peter Peterson and wife came home with us from church—Peter is a cousin of the Nelson girls. They stayed to supper—went to church from here and came back for coffee & cake after church. Pete says that Jim Nelson has purchased a farm in Dakota and will move in the spring. The next evening there was nothing extra on. Then Tues & Wed evenings I was at meeting and Thurs I went to Harlan with Mr. Scott. Mrs Jensen taught school for me that day so I wont have to make it up on Saturday.

Dr Weber wasn't satisfied with any more than I was he said the medicine wasn't strong enough and that I would have to take several months more treatment. I paid him and said I couldn't afford any more treatment and he said he [would] finish the treatment for nothing so here goes. he also said he found something wrong with my hearing when he examined my ears and he told me how to treat them and if they do not improve he thinks an operation would be necessary but I think they are improving. He was to send me some other medicine and glasses. he sent them to Irwin. I got a card from Dr Weber saying he had expressed the package so I spoke to the mailman about bringing it out he said he would but would have to wait for the card from the express company and have me sign it. I ask about charges and he looked foolish and said he wouldn't charge me anything—Say he isn't married.

I didn't go to meeting that evening I came home from Harlan but went Friday evening, then Saturday I did my ironing wrote some letters and did some mending then went home with Anna Sorensen the dress maker who has been staying with her cousin and her cousins were away and Walter Christensen a cousin of the Petersen children has been doing chors so Charlie went over too, and the four of us *kids* had a great time. All went to church Sunday morning and there were four boys here for dinner and till church time in the evening Oh yes! the Friday before there was some one here in the evening after church and we all played—that game that Harrises[1] play I can't spell it.

Say I received a long delayed Xmas present a few days ago—a box of writing paper am sending sample of same. Guess it came from Neb. but dont know.

This is below zero and Im up stairs—my fingers are so stiff I must quit. Couldn't get a team Sat. and don't know about next Sat. please write.

Elizabeth Corey
Irwin Iowa

1. Benjamin and Emma Harris, parents of Valerie, Orla, and Glen, lived catty-corner from the Corey family (PG). Says Paul Corey, "We were on the northwest, they on the southeast, the schoolhouse on the southwest" (CMW).

. . . .

JANUARY 19, 1908 IRWIN, IOWA

To Mrs. E. O. Corey

Dear Mamma,—Did you get my letter written Wed. evening? Havent heard so will write a little more. I went to church Thurs. & Fri. evenings. The grate went to pieces in the school stove so I had to go over to the directors after school—Sorine and Millie Scott visited school Friday afternoon so Sorine went over to Christensens with me. Saturday we got up late. I wrote letters before noon and as I wished to get a money order—went out to talk to the mail man. Klinke said to send stamps so I sent stamps. I told him I thought mailmen were supposed to charge for carrying packages he said they were supposed to but he didn't have the nerve to charge a girl—said he would do most any thing for a girl. He tried to tease me about some of the mail I've been getting till I felt like telling him I thought he had plenty of nerve and that it took him an awful long time to count a few stamps but after counting ten held my piece.

In the afternoon cleaned my schoolhouse and helped Mrs Scott some. Myrtle went over to her Aunt Hannahs—*we* told her just to see Walter Christensen and she said that was what she was going for so we had to smile at supper time when four young people that Myrtle is much interested in came in to spend the evening. They left a little after twelve and the funny part of it was they all invited Charlie and I to come and see them or rather invited us to come and spend the evening but hardly mentioned Myrtle.

We went to church as usual this morning and had a whole house full of company this after noon—three families—one family from Marne who will stay alnight they are all at church now but me. I am not at all well tonight—just feel horrid and such a head ache—they told me that I look pale but they just imagine that but my eyes are inflamed and painful. I went upstairs after the crowd started to leave and slept for a couple of hours—off and on—sort of cat naps you know. After they were all gone to church I did all the bedroom work— three beds and so on—up stairs—didn't have time this morning as I had to take a bath—then I cleared the supper table and washed the dishes and now if I can get this finished before they get back I'll do well.

I don't see much hopes of getting home for a long long time— There is a box social at the center next Friday evening and the spelling contest the next day and the next Friday evening there is the County Spelling Contest in Harlan and teachers meeting next day. I'll send you my spair chink when I get some.

Say is it right to let young men I'm not much acquainted with call me Bessie? Hans Petersen called me Bessie last night I guess he got that from the Scott girls but he is such a nice kid and was my partner so much of the time I didn't like to call him down.

You know the yarns that Chris was telling the boys? Well I've heard some that beat those all to pieces.

Am going to inclose a stamp picture of Charlie Peterson one of my good boys and a drawing by Chris Nelson another of my good boys.

I must close hoping to hear from you soon I am

Your Little Girl

Bess

[At top of first page:] please send back picture.

[Enclosure: A postage-stamp sized photograph of Charlie Peterson but no drawing]

* *

FEBRUARY 1, 1908 IRWIN, IOWA

To Mrs. E. O. Corey, Elmdale

Dear Ma,—Yours rec'd yesterday and contents noted.

I'm sure I dont know where I left of but there has been two or three evenings that I've been at home and didn't have company

One evening Alice and Fred Berger were here and one evening Edna Jensen was here, Sorine was here and stayed alnight with me and Marie was here over night once and Martha & Chris Nelson were here to see *me* one evening and I was at Rev Jensens one evening at Nelsons one evening and at Soren Scotts one Sunday. Mrs Nelson and Mrs Berger visited school one day this week and Martha visited school one day last week. I had hoped to be able to go to Harlan the last of this week. There was Dr Weber Thurs. Exams Fri. Spelling Contest Fri. eve. and teachers meeting today.

Did you know Lida Smith is teaching in Harlan? has charge of a class room I don't see any show of getting home before—well goodness knows when for though there is lots going on here all the time there is no way of getting out of the neighborhood it seems.

Please send me some celery salt next time you write.

Are you feeling much better? Robert and Josephene want you to come back there next summer and stay a long time they want you to come there first and then they will take you to see the rest of the folks and surprise them.

She said they were coming out here as soon as they could but the baby was too small to bring Xmas and she said she did write me last and has been wondering all the while what ailed me that I didn't write.

I suppose Dell & Bert have sailed ere this. Yess Olney said he would never marry a "Lilliputian" as he would always have to be carrying a chair around for her to stand on to kiss him or he would have to be continuely doubling up like a jack-knife which would give him a stitch in the back. But he didn't turn pale—he didn't know she was here till she came into the room and stood right beside him and then oh how red he got—clear down to his collar.

I've been reading School Law. I think I am right guess I'll mail you a piece. Whats up? been scraping the little school maam?

Shall I send you this months wages? Mrs Scott will wait for board and I have plenty to last a while without.

Well I must close and write some buisness letters.

Yours as ever

Bess

. . . .

FEBRUARY 16, 1908 IRWIN, IOWA

To Mrs. E. O. Corey

Dear Ma,—Last Sunday evening when I finished my letter to Chall it was about half after eleven. the next evening I had some mending to do and the next evening I went home with Rose Sherlock after school—had a fine time—Mr Sherlock is in the Asylum at Clarinda—four of the children go to school to me and there are four who dont go to school they are to have a sale tomorrow and go to Neb. the last of the week to live near her folks. They have rented their farm here—Ralph the eldest son is a little older than Fuller and very much such a boy too—after much coaxing he played for me on the violin—some of the tunes Fuller plays—and he is fond of dancing and knows the violinists from your neighbor hood who play about here. He is as interested in machinery as Fuller and his greatest ambition is to invent a machine that will run by air or run itself so to speak—but as he is a farmer *like Fuller* he has little time

I was also much interested in "Johnie" who is a real cute lad of sixteen who insisted on bringing us to school as it was muddy and would hear to no thanks but said as he leaned back after handing me my dinner bucket "I wish you would come back again." Well I received three very interesting letters and two very interesting post cards also my check and two other post cards.

I went up to Jeppe Nelsons Thurs evening to stay all night with Martha who is about my age—much like Ida Wever and one of the best girls that ever lived. Had a fine time but didn't get acquainted with her brothers at all as they are all so bashful and so am I, you know. Three of them hardly spoke to me but Roy told me Friday morning at breakfast that I was going to get a *lot* of Valentines but I guess he didn't know as I only got one but that one is a stunner I went home with Sorine Scott Friday evening. Saturday morning we went to Poplar and in the after noon started my dress. Hans Petersen was there most all day and teased us all by turns—presisted on whistling "Sweet Bunch of Daises" and calling me Bessie although I told him that my mother said I wasn't to let any one call me Bessie because it sounded too too you know. We sewed up to supper time then after supper made some calls and I didn't come home till this morning on the way to church.

We had company this after noon—and we all went to church this evening—One of my pupils and another young man were babtised— something I never saw before. The floor of the pulpit raises up and underneath is a large tank in which they placed several barrels of water Friday. One corner of church they had curtained off for a dressing room then after the regular services the minister and the young men entered the dressing room while two men moved the chairs and lifted the pulpit floor then the minister went down the steps into the water and held out his hand and one young man came out walked down and knelt on the step—after certain services were gone through with he tipped him backward down down into the tank then he got out and went into the dressing room with the water just streaming off of him and the other lad came out and went through the same boooooo can't you just hear my teeth rattle now?

The roads were too bad for us this week but if possible there will be a whole load of us down next Friday evening—the rest of them wish to spend Saturday with some friend in Marne Don't worry about keeping them over night as they will just put up with any thing if you will let them come.

Well it is getting awful late and I haven't been feeling very well so must ring off and go to roost.

You might call me up after you get this—my how I would like to hear every thing from down there.

How is Bert Line? And are Hainses well? Bye Bye,

Your little girl Bess.

. . . .

MARCH 7, 1908 IRWIN, IOWA

To Mrs. M. M. Corey

Dear Ma,—I dont see what ailed me when I wrote that last letter I didn't tell you half but I'm going to start this tonight and mail it Monday and perhaps I'll get most of it in this time.

Two of my big boys quit school last Monday—C__ was one of them of course—poor kid he don't have an easy time of it and thats a cinch. I guess its so about what you said. C__ and I started to read "Cast Up By The Sea"[1] together the week after we were down there and some one else started to read it right away too. Well you can guess about how it was—Charlie stoped school Monday—helped a neighbor all day and then M[artin Scott] sent him after a load of straw just at dark and he had his usual amt. to do afterwards. Of course it was late before he got through milking. For a wonder M run the separater and so C__ washed for supper and got the book then vat you tink? C__ had to go down and feed calves though M hadn't done anything all day but attend School Meeting. Mrs. S[2] was *gol* and said what she thought when the rest were not around. The next day C__ hid the book so when we wanted it we didn't have to wait on anyone. Oh well I guess *we* wont read any more books.

C__ was going to try to finish school this Spring. I was going to help him out of school—His mother had quite set her heart on it but when C__ saw how matters stood he said he could see no hope ahead and we'd have to give it up so we did, though he says he dont believe he'll get to go to school a day next winter. C__ don't say much but I guess he alows to keep his acounts balanced.

I got a great long letter from Ida [Weaver] a week ago—it had been opened though there was no explanation of it and Polly Wally claims to know nothing of it. Polly Wally promised last Saturday to bring me some unruled letter paper the first of this week but it didn't show up so today I went out and roasted him about the opened letter which he declared he hadn't noticed. then I went after him about the writing paper which he had completely forgotten he was very penitent—called himself a blockhead and so on—said he would go down town and get it tonight and bring it out Monday—As I turned to come to the house he said the roads were "ricadudalus" today and then for the first time I knew what had been ailing the Polk T'w'p roads the past week.

Ida's letter was full of news good-bad-and "middlin"—she is attending Buisness College at Salem and doing well—has a steady beau—and the other Sunday P.M. when he was to see her they were in the sitting room and as the clock struck five Lee burst into the room with the exclamation "Its ten oclock, man, you better go home" and she says thats just a sample of his actions. Gertie had a baby boy born Jan 11. it was dead—never made a sound. G__ has been having a frightful time with gathered breasts has had one lanced once and the other twice—had been over for Mrs Wever to care for, two weeks when Ida wrote.

Tell Rob I appreciated that pretty Post Card but we are not going to have a social—thought from the way the rest turned out around here it wouldn't pay but they say for Rob to come up anyway. I guess the children enjoyed their visit down there—I ask Charlie if what happened Saturday morning spoiled his visit and he said "Well I guess not!" that he had hardly thought of it again till I mentioned it—the girls know nothing of it and he said he would do as he'd be done by and never mention it to any one. Mrs S and Myrtle say Charlie often speaks of the "Dandy pudding Mrs Corey can make out of her own head" he declares its better than anything before or since and one day when he was having a time with a piece of beaf he remarked that it wasn't like what we had at Coreys

Today was Myrtles birthday, she was fifteen. We've all worked to make her have a good time and I guess she has had a day of it. Mrs S sent her up stairs to make beds and wanted to phone to some of the girls to come over but was afraid M__ would hear so Gordon and I went up to "help" her and made such a noise and teased her so that she didn't hear anything and how surprised she was when the girls came in by two's and threes and how they all laughed when we told about it—We had roast goose and the "trimmins" for dinner and chocolate and cake this P.M.

Say ma could you send me Ethels measure? you can put it down beside the one enclosed and return it. take the measure snug an I'll see to the rest—have that old gray skirt to make over if I have time.

If Rob comes up please send a set of Jack Stones out of the machine[3] drawer I received a letter from C. H. Christensen offering me this school for the Spring what do you think about it? I have five more weeks here any way.

Well good night—I'll finish this tomorrow

March 8—Well I'm not a oncer having been to church twice today— had company all afternoon.

This morning C was dressing in the sitting room and came to the door and explained to Gordon that he had forgot and left his Sunday pants up stairs in the south room by the door and wanted G to go after them but G wouldn't so I said I would C__ was still for an instant and then exclamed "You Dane!" in a tone that causes me to laugh when I think of it. At dinner C was telling the crowd that if I was here much longer I would know every word in Dane and Mrs S said C came to her this morning and said "Oh mamma what shall we do. we cant talk Dane any more with out her knowing all about it— she understands every word" It amused them all and we have lots of fun about it.

We had some music this after noon Millie played and part of the time Millie and C and I and M sang and part of the time just I and Martin sang

Well it is growing late and I had better close hoping that financial affairs are turning out well and that you will have a happy birthday I am

Your Little Girl

Bess

Tell Rob to come up Fri Mar 13

[Written across the top of the first page:] Take care of this letter *mum.*

1. *Cast Up by the Sea* by Sir Samuel W. Baker, first published England in 1869, is an adventure-filled romance with a plot that rests upon a confusion of parentage consequent to a shipwreck. Its chief interest for readers of our own day might

be its graphic account of a slave raid upon an African village or perhaps the author's casual use of the epithet *nigger* in the same sense as Bess employs it in her own writings.

2. Mrs. Scott.

3. Sewing machine.

. . . .

APRIL 7, [1908] IRWIN, IOWA

To Mrs. E. O. Corey

Dear Ma,—Yours rec'd last Friday and it most knocked the socks off of me though had expected it for months especialy since Xmas. I got your letter at Recess and by four oclock was almost sick but got over it when I cooled off a little and realized that God would care for you and the rest of us too

Myrtle will patch it up with Rob about those jackstones

I wish the seed corn had tested better but—one good thing about testing it that way is you don't need to use any but good ears.

Yes Ive heard from Lida—just Saturday—she is teaching John Lamers school four miles from you—says Hank Lamers are out of a teacher and its too bad, "an ideal school you know." And Mary Lanagan writes that the school two miles east of the home school is out yet too. I just signed my contract this morn.

If Jno. Backsons lawyer comes too near just give him a "hoopie big time"

Sunday evening Millie and I were comming home from church. we were overtaken by "Bud" Snider and "Pussy" Tage who stopped and ask us to ride—Millie knew them and would have rode but I didn't know them so I thanked them saying the distance was so short and we were so near it wasn't worth while—we refused them point blank three times before they went on. If you was me would you have rode? Well I just thought "No "blasted" Buds for me—how do I know they would let us out at the corner?" And beside we had turned them down once before.

Next is about Polly Wally and oh ma it just seems as if fate had thrown him at my head ever since I came up here and now—Well first it was express, then it was the "Cousin John" joke, then it was Hypockets, then he got the unruled writing paper I couldn't get at

Poplar, then I rec'd a letter with "postage due" written on it, which he had paid and brought out without a word, then once he said he "thought it would snow—wished it would and that he might come down and take me sleigh riding Sunday," and geting Money orders and stamps and the like Ive seen him quite frequently so Saturday as I was too stiff to walk to town I though[t] of another way to get my order cashed. it was the mailmans brother who came Saturday so I gave him the order for his brother to cash and bring me the money Monday—well he gave it to the mailman Sunday morning and he put the envelope with it in in his hip pocket. after choreing around the stable (he owns the livery stable) all forenoon the envelope and order were missing. He looked for it from then till dark but didn't find it so Monday morning he notified the Irwin & Harlan banks by 'phone. He left no word concerning it Mon. I didn't think much about that, supposing the money would be left Tuesday so today Charlie went out to palm himself off as my guardean and take care of the money. It was a very serious mailman who told him the whole story of the order with many regrets He said he had never lost a letter or anything else out of his hip pocket in his life and never thought of such a thing and would much rather have lost ten dollars. I'll get the duplicate as soon as possible and get the money but I dont like the delay—I had thought I could spare five or perhaps ten to boost Olney—would have been such a nice birthday present but its too late now.

I have all my letters answered but the five I got last week and this is one of them.

Does Robert remember the man who was here the first night he was? Well that was Mr Hikeaway well last Saturday evening about eight oclock when every one here had almost finished a desperately hard weeks work they got word that the Hikeways from Cuppies Grove would be here for over night—well I thought the whole family were going to sit down and bawl but they rallied and we finished supper and cleared up in time to get supper for the other crowd.— The other crowd arrived about nine oclock and there was Paw Hikeway and Maw Hikeway and I counted *one, two, three, four, five,* then stepped inside the sitting room to ask Charlie how many little Hikes there were any way. he named them [on] his fingers fourteen I think there was but they weren't all here. They are the queerest crowd I ever saw—it was most two much for me in spite of Charlies warnings. C & I couldn't look at each other all evening without our "faces hurting" as C says. We went in the sitting room and gave 'em music to eat by—made it fast so there would be something left for breakfast. Then we planed for half an hour in the shadow of the cupboard door to find some way to sleep 'em all without hanging 'em on hooks. I tryed to learn their names theres Minnie Crysanthemum and Juleas Ceaser and Agnes and Lillian and a Niels Christian and a Arthur— something and there I lost out. Of course they were going to church (Sunday morn) and I thought "My stars!! if they are going with our crowd we've got to do something!" So while Myrtle scrubbed the kids faces I hunted out hair ribbons some of which I will never see again except in my dreams—there were white for Lillian blue for Agnes and my beloved black bow for Minnie. Then we combed their hair & glorymareau! such a mess Minnies was about eight inches long and like hog bristles. I dont believe it had ever known a straight part but after much work a pair of my side combs, hair pins and black bow it looked much like other girls' hair. Myrtle gave her a waist so we were most satisfied with our work.

Charlie didn't go to church thats unusual for him but perhaps that was to rest his face.

The little Hikes took quite a liking to the schoolmaam and I completely won the hearts of Paw & Maw Hike by "kindness" to the little Hikes and Oh ma the little Hikes used to go to school to Lida at Cuppys Grove though I didn't know it till they were gone.

A week ago Sunday I went with the Scott girls to Chris Christensens over west of here where Hans Petersen works—had never met any of the folks but had a fine time we got weighed—Sorine weighed 217 and I 201 or more than twenty less than I weighed last fall. And every one around here says I'm getting thin but I can't see it only my duds are getting too big.

I felt awful bum last week but feel better now my eyes haven't hurt much today but are beginning to and as it is nearing twelve will close hoping this will find you better I am

Your Little Girl

Bess

One of the two Easter cards Bess sent her family in 1908.

APRIL 14, 1908 IRWIN, IOWA

To Mrs. E. O. Corey & Family

[A pair of lithographed Easter postcards printed in Germany, embossed and in full color. One card displays a mother hen watching her three yellow, freshly hatched chicks; the other card displays a flamboyantly feathered rooster observing, with some consternation, a similar setting of brightly colored eggs. Each card carries on its face the words "Easter Greeting" in red, but on its back the card is blank, Bess apparently intending that the cards convey their own holiday message to her family. The cards are contained in a single, addressed envelope identical to those currently in use for Bess's letters.]

APRIL 21, 1908 IRWIN, IOWA

To Mrs. M. M. Corey

Dear Ma,—It is about ten P.M. but am going to write you any way for if I put it off much longer I fear you will have to pay extra postage or does your mail man pay it for you?

Well lets see—about three weeks ago was at a birthday party a[t] Bergers and two weeks ago I spent the evening at Jeppe Nelsons and a week ago last Sat. I was in Harlan—had almost given up all hopes of getting a chance to go when Sorine came down to tell me her father had to go to mill and might go along. (You see she couldn't phone for *we* were house cleaning—painted kitchen three coats and one pantz and couldn't use the phone for over a week.) so I got ready and took my Duplicate Order along. We didnt get started till quite late and it took us between four & five hours to get there—drove the old white mules Petra the Liliplution went along for company and pushed on one line while I pushed on the other and Mr Scott walked along side most of the way to use the whip to better advantage. It was half after two before we got there and then I had to visit a shoe store, milinare store, bookstore, drygoods store, jewelers and dentists so didn't have any time to throw away. Had to get hat jacket and other things too numerous to mention—suppose your hair will raise when I tell you I spent between twenty five and thirty dollars but *then* I didn't get quite all I needed. Well we left town about half after six and got to Soren Scotts about half after eleven and I was home and most ready for bed by twelve.

The following Monday a week ago yesterday I opened my Spring term of school—have *two* new pupils making nineteen in all. And the same day Myrtle went to work for her Aunt Hannah.

Wednesday afternoon I dismissed school to attend the funeral of Elmer Larsen who died of Lung fever after an illness of three weeks— his brother Harry is very low with the same. I was some what acquainted with the family having spent one evening there and Harry spent one evening here besides meeting them elsewhere. Elmer was eighteen and was near enough like Fuller in size, looks, disposition and tastes to have been his twin brother.

Wednesday evening I went to prayer meeting at John Mortensens and made the acquaintance of Mr Eugene Dunham the teacher from two miles north who *wished* to make my acquaintance last winter. I find that his parents live near Salem Mo. not far from Wevers though having not been home much this last year he is not personly acquainted with them Mr Dunham is medium highth, well built, quite dark, has the soft musical voice, easy grace and southern politeness you read about in books—he was reared in luxury then thrown upon his own resources but he is as independant as a hog on ice and has more pride than you could boil down two to one and put in a vinegar barrel. I tell you ma I'm struck this time and got it bad—why since Wednesday evening the grass murmers Mr Dunham, the trees whisper Mr Dunham, the birds sing Mr Dunham, the wind howls Mr Dunham, and the chickens, mamma, even the chickens, why there's one darned old hen that stands before my window and screams "Schooldad Dunham Schooldad Dunham Schooldad Dunham" while an ornery old rooster stands on one foot and answers in surprise "From Missouri well I never" Till I might throw the lamp and every thing else I could get my hands on at them if I wasn't afraid of having another racket with the Missus.—had one—it lasted from Wed. till the end of the week—was called most of the pro*nounc*eable names from liar and tattle tale down. Twice I went up stairs and bawled till I looked like a beery dutchman but its all over now peace has been restored and we can all smile once more

Oh I forgot to tell you about my visit to the Dentist. He said it was an "impacked wisdom" one of the worst kind they ever had to pull he said he would have to file off a portion before he could pull it and it had been left so long it had started the next one to it to decay.

He asked me which I wished to take gass or chloraform and I said I had never taken either. He looked at me a minute then said he would at least inject some thing into the gums to deaden it a little as there was no use in any one being tortured so. I didnt think it was much deadened a little later but got through it pretty well.

Say you know how snug the belt of my black skirt was when I came up here well it laps over a fingers length now. I'm going to fatten up some so you'll know me when I get home.

When I looked over Ethels measurements I thought she was too big a girl to fit by guess, so have attempted nothing but an apron which I started last evening it is all done but part of the buttons and button holes which I will finish in the morning.

Yesterday I got a nice letter from Cairo Neb., signed "One of your schoolkids"—the second, a *very* pretty postal mailed in Irwin. Charlie & I have compared the writing with all we could get ahold of but find no clew and there are no initials or any mark to identify the sender. I also rec'd a letter from Florence Brown, Nourmals wife. Nourmal would like to have one of the boys come down an help him this summer as he cannot find a hand.

Rec'd a letter from Ida last Saturday telling the sad news of Walter Millers death from Pneumonia April 4th. His father never sent for a doctor till just the evening before he died. Ida said she should have thought one dose of that would have been enough for Miller.

When Robert comes up I wish he would drive and bring my suit case packed with all of my summer underwear thats any account and my blue kitchen skirt—then he can take back the valice with my coat fur and other winter duds

Well the roosters are crowing so I must close hoping to hear the latest from home I will say Goodnight

I overslept this morning. so long to you

Your Little Girl

Bess

• •

MAY 6, 1908 IRWIN, IOWA

To Mrs. M. M. Corey

Dear Mamma,—I fear you will not like my writing paper—have been out and waited some time for this.

Well Im up a tree and the dog still growls. You know my school closes June 19 and Summer School commences June 22 so I just have an over Sunday vacation, which is short considering—well everything you know

It will take you a week to read this for I'm most daffy I don't know where to begin and I suppose it will be like the boarding house hash H. H. Armstrong tells about.

Sunday just before Rob started home C and I were scrapping—he was going to set me in a chair but he didn't—well I got rather warm and when Rob was getting ready to start off I was out doors quite a bit and rode a piece with him most half a mile—I thought I had cooled off plenty before I left the house I didn't feel warm so didnt wear a wrap. Shortly after I got back I was taken with severe pains through my limbs and back—guess Mrs Scott thought I was going to have spinal mengitis (don't suppose that was spelled right) that frightful disease so many have died with lately for that is just the way theyer taken I guess—well about six I gave it up as a bad job and went to bed. Mrs Scott rubbed me with some kind of hot stuff dosed me with hot lemonade and put on an extra quilt so I was soon almost roasting and by Monday morning felt pretty good—only as sore as a boil all over.

Was up last night & stayed alnight with my dressmaker—am going Saturday to stay a week with her and get my sewing done—might as well have it done first as last for my eyes wont stand the racket.

All the plumb juices are mine aren't they? Yah! Yah!

Rec'd a joehimmy of a postal from Ida Monday and a letter from Lida today. it was a stunner—she dared me to let C__ read it but I guess I wont. I have nineteen pupils and *Mrs Scott has* six little goslings—oh my goodness no, its the old goose that has 'em—guess thats equal to the fifty one little pigs.

I did think once that I wouldn't have any more washing done till I came home but now I think I will have my sewing washing ironing and mending done before I go home. so all I will have to do will be to repack. But oh how I wish I could see Ethel and Paul off to Atlantic Olney off to Okla and you off to Omaha befor I go I could feel so much more easy. When are you planning on going? You will be able to use the new suit case to advantage wont you? I suppose the little school ma'am can give you all necessary pointers as to what duds and things you will need to take alone I wouldn't have any idea would you?

I will be able to send Ethel her blue longsleaved apron some time soon I hope. What other sewing will you have to have done for her?

How did Toad like that postal? It reminded me of the time he said that he and his girl had been in swimming.

Is Mary going to Summer School? I wish we could be close together but I would kind of like to stay at Smiths if they would take me.

Our teachers meeting was called for this evening but eight miles walk over these roads was to much for me to think of—might have taken advantage of leap year and called up Schooldad Dunham and talked it over

Will close hoping to hear some of your plans soon I am
Your Little Girl
Bess.

MAY 17, 1908 IRWIN, IOWA

To Mrs. M. M. Corey

Dear Mamma,—This is Sunday eve about ten o'clock so here goes but I dont know where to begin—have forgoten whether I told you about prayer meeting at Langlands or not.

A week ago Friday evening I was to go up to Soren Scotts to board for a week while Sorine did some sewing for me—Mr Scott, Sorines father, was taken sick the Sat. before, nothing serious they thought then, but by the time I got there he was so bad they had had the doctor and she said it was *quite* serious so I told Sorine I would go back and wait if she thought best but she said to stay for she had put me off so long already so I staid alnight and she sewed for me Saturday. Saturday noon her father got worse and for awhile we thought every breath would be his last I would have come home on towards evening but the girls begged me to stay with them so I did, and came home Sunday morning. Mr M[artin] Scott phoned down here to Mrs S. that if she wished to see his father again alive to come at once. Before noon they phoned for I and the boys to come, so we did. Mr Scott seems to be improving in some ways but not in others.

There was no church here that forenoon on account of storm but Charlie and I went in the evening

Martha was down to visit School one after noon this week and staid till six in the evening—had a nice visit

Mrs Scott was away one eve so I got supper—had it ready at the usual time—Mrs S had told Charlie to get it but he didn't feel bad because I got ahead of him. C was to go after his mother that is she said he was to come after her—Gordon had run off and C and I were most done supper when M came in, and I ask him if he was going after Mrs S he looked queer and said yes if C wasnt going I answered cool as a cucumber that I guessed Charlie wasn't going. C took the hint so it was Mr S who went and C who staid.

Friday eve I went up for Sorine to fit a dress, (she has been sewing some the last few days) and I hadn't been there long befor Mr S came up and betwixt and between them all *We* walked home together

Saturday afternoon was up again and I guess I wont have to board there at all now.

Have just five more weeks of School now and am doing well—

nearly all have completed this years work and now have time for a *strong* review—that is good considering the irregular attendance. Did I tell you M. C. visited school one day and addressed the children, said I was doing good work, was quite taken with that reception we gave to parents and friends and was altogether *lovely*?

Saturday afternoon Mrs and Mr Scott were in town, I washed out my handkerchieves and scrubbed the kitchen and it *was a job*. Mrs S was pleased to find it scrubbed, and so was I when Mr Sam Christensen of Council Bluffs arrived for an over Sunday visit.

Was at church this morning. It rained this afternoon so there was no services this evening

I'm desperately blue, homesick and lonesome some times and find my Bible a great comfort but you must not think I'm so very bad off for Mrs S has been very kind to me of late and I certainly have my share of all the fun going and on reflection I think I've done exceptionly well.

You must not plan on any more of my money this Spring for I've been at quite a little expense and am planning on Summer School— have written to Mary L to see if she wont go in with me so we can hire a room and board our selves as it is much cheaper I wish you and Mary would talk it over and I wish you would write me your plans for the Summer—I have no vacation before Summer S but I think you should have that operation as soon as possible after school is out down there—I could go up to see you the Fourth.

Have rec'd three postals and two letters this week but cant under stand the joke about the chickens or who the card is from

Was very sorry to miss seeing Mrs Bradly but you cant expect me home till June 19.

Your Little Girl Bess

. . . .

MAY 26, 1908 IRWIN, IOWA

To Mrs. Margaret M. Corey

Dear Ma,—I have more to do this evening than I can possibly get done so thought I would write to you first.

I hope this letter wont make you sick though I expect it will be rather gloomy as I'm feeling *very blue* (in spots) and, like F[uller], am rather disgusted with this corner of the world. Myrtle and the boys got home from Harlan last evening—Myrtle is rooming with me this week—I dont mind making the bed and hanging up duds and could stand the racket if she would "*carry it out*" but suppose I must make the best of a bad bargan. Am feeling well but am rather stiff in the shoulders [added in pen above the line: stiff in the joints, Paul would say] and have had a sick headache yesterday afternoon and today, and tell the Little Schoolmaam that the chickens have changed their tune and now that old hen stops in her daily promanade on the schoohouse step to call tauntingly in at the door "Broncho-buster, Brochobuster, how'd you like it? how'd you like it?" While the rooster stands in a flower bed and says, "Whoa Fanny." [added in pen:] *The horrid old thing.*

This picnic will be anything but a picnic for me—work and expense before and after and a world of care for the day.

Tell F that Andersons say to bring the halter up next time he comes

Marten went to Pine Creek near Independance Iowa to attend conference went last evening Sorine and Millie were down for the evening—staid late which didn't improve my headache any.

You know these folks belong to a meat route or club or what you may call it—well its their turn to butcher—will butcher this evening and Mr Strong the butcher will be here over night Sorine is here already she is going to help the boys take the meat around and she wanted to get here in time to make a mash on the butcher she said—am going to sit in the shade and watch the fun—don't dare *say* anything or I'll get *canned*

Hope you are all well and Mrs B still improving with best regards to all I'll close for now and write more before mailing perhaps

Bess

Thurs May 29—Guess I'll try to finish this before school time.

Sunday eve we got here at eleven—before Mr—Mrs Scott. Monday eve the children came home from Rolds and Martin went to Conference. Tuesday night the butcher stayed alnight here Wednesday I staid alnight with Sorine and last evening I spent the evening at Jeppe Nelsons and stayed alnight at M C Jensens. Mrs Scott says "I do like your brother Fuller just awful well"—a very extraordinary speech for that lady.

Picnic will be a fizzle I *guess*

You might tell Mary L__ I'm ready to call off that plan I suggested and if I can get in at Gillets or some where else I'll not go Smiths so there now.

There were about fourteen other things I wished to mention but no more for now from E. F. C.

[another page added:] Here goes for another instalment I wanted to tell you that Sorine didn't make much of an impression on the butcher—she was *very* nice and I sat between Charlie and Mrs S__ and was very proper except spilling the potatoes, my glass of water & talking half Dane and half English and a few other brakes I couldn't resist putting in an answer once in a while.—While the other girls went down to watch the butchering process I went to bed It is realy funny but I do believe *I* made more of an impression than Sorine though *I* didnt *dint* him *much.*

Mrs S__ calls me "Bessie." Wouldn't that frieze you?

I was very sorry to notice that F__ was so dissatisfied and yet its no wonder but can't you make some little change? F__ thinks that perhaps he and Chall could get along with the work, and couldn't Rob work out and share up some with F__ or couldn't F__ work out and pay for the extra help at home he would like to try it and if O[lney] stays at home and works by the day it would be a good thing for him. He has a notion he would like to get away from home and if he could I think it would be a good thing for him—he would find that weeds will grow in the best of fields.

I would so like to help F__ out financialy but I fear I will run short as it is before the summer is over. Tell Toad so please

So long

Bess

[written in the side margin of page 4:] am feeling fine but am about half blind some of the time.

[Written sideways at the bottom of the letter:] Now for goodness sake let *every one* read this letter its so *lovely*

. . . .

MAY 31, 1908 IRWIN, IOWA

To Mrs. M. M. Corey

Dear Ma,—My last letter to you is still in the mail box but notwithstanding, nevertheless I'll start another at once I wrote Fern a letter in which I chronicled the joys and sorrows of Friday and Saturday you can ring her to find out about our team for the picnic and why I'm not such a hard drinker as in former years. My order also came home from Harlan uncashed so I'm in it another once.

I didn't tell Fern though that Sorines fellow stopped to talk to me on the road up to Scotts to take Sorine to Decoration Day exercises in Harlan and suggested that I go instead of Sorine. Oh if Sorine could have overheard *that* wouldn't she have killed us both? It was realy worse than when she got to Chatauqua and saw Earl K and I together You know this fellow is the one that found the piece of my glasses and brought it over to me.

We all went to church this morning and after church Sorine and Millie stopped for dinner. They wanted Myrtle and I to go down to Larsens with them this afternoon—Mrs S[cott] wouldn't let M[artin] go as they were all going over to Aunt Hannahs and she said if she was me she wouldn't go so I went over to Aunt Hannahs with the rest which made Sorine awful "*gol*." Walter was over there too and had his magazine rifle its just a stunner. He let me shoot at a mark on a box with it and I missed the mark two inches and wasn't a rod away I dont believe. At first the boys wondered at my daring to shoot and then marveled at my hitting the box at all.[1] Walter gave me the empty shell to "Remember the occasion by." He said he'd be over here again before I went home. Now what do you think of that?

I most forgot to tell you I worked button holes in two black waists and sewed the buttons on them yesterday afternoon which just about played my eyes out completely—they have been *very* bad this week.

Marie Jensen was down for over night last night and borrowed the last three books I brought from home for her and Edna to read—both girls plan on a visit to my home with the two bookcases of books, *some time.*

When I got home from Aunt Hs I was so blue and homesick I hardly knew where I was at. I asked C__ what was a cure for home-sickness and he said "go home." A cure of another kind came before dark in the shape of the Hikeaways—there was just Mr. Hikeaway, Mrs Hikeaway and one little Hike so this eve has been tame com-pared with the one when the Mr and Mrs and *six* little Hikes were here It was just chore time when they arrived so I was left to entertain the Mrs & little Hike but I managed it fine showed the little Hike a picture like I gave the children for the last day of school and told him he might take it home with him—then gave him a piece of candy to suck. While he was busy at that I aired my best Danish and Mrs Hike aired her best English and we got on—oh "I cant 'spress it in English," you know.

I scrubbed my hair last eve which makes it very fluffy—it is trying its best to curl but hasn't succeeded very well so far.

Most every one tells me these days that I'm getting thin but I cant see it—am eating like sixty though—two meals aday and some times three

Well as I must go to puppy town tomorrow evening after school (four mile walk) an am also doing extra work in school will close for now.

Good Night

From Bess

P.S. The Hikes are still talking—Sounds like bumblebees in a jug. E. F. C.

Monday June 1.

Didn't sleep very well last night and this morning my right ankle which I turned coming home from church yesterday was swolen and painful—Put in rather a trying day take it all around—The directors Young Hopeful was as ornery as sin all day—kept him after school—ignored his presence entirely—finished my work about five o'clock—took my key and took several steps toward the door when I heard a very audible sniff—an hour is a long time for a youngster who is waiting, like Johnny Brown, to "Have it over with" and then the idea of locking him in for over night was too much for the little rat and he came to time at once "Will never never do it any more." You know if I'd let him go home to his ma this once—Wonder how he'll be tomorrow

Asked the mailman today if I could trust him with another money order and he reached for it assuring me that I *could* trust him if I just would and he would take the best kind of care of it Then after he was up the road a ways I discovered he had only taken part of the letters and postals that were to mail so I called to him and then took the letters etc to him—didnt loose my dignity and run though—good thing I didn't for the boys are after me any way about running up the road to catch the mail man have known from the first I intended "To catch him" and so on

My but this candy I'm eating is good (?) hot as blazes—boys just came up—stopped on the road to give me some—said it was fine. Oo ha!!!

Rec'd a postal to day—picture of Pearl St. looking North Council Bluffs there was quite a little on the correspondance side signed—From Mr Hypokits C. B., I. it was mailed at Kirkman and I just know it was from Hans Petersen for we have had so much fun over Hans' friend Mr Hypockits—Hans used to live in the Bluffs.

Didnt go to puppy town tonight for various reasons so will have that tomorrow eve.

Martin Scott came home from Conferance this evening and I heard *some thing* of which, more later as it wont do to write but for once I've helped C get even in a way that counted

Good Night

From Bess

Saturday June 6

Will try and write a little more before the mail man comes It rained Monday night and Tues forenoon so Charlie went to puppy town for me Tues afternoon and got the ribbon for our badges and such a time as I had lettering them—ink and paint blured so at last I had to work the letters on—will inclose the one I wore if I dont forget it. They were a fright to work. I could hardly see straight when I got through with them

The weather was so changeable we decided not to take a rack but went in three carriage loads and just at the last moment Mr Berger wouldn't let his "kids" go so Carl Jensen didn't either and that knocked our share of the programe all in the head. My dont I love that Mr Berger good and proper!! He is always doing me or some one else just such a good turn that why he is so popular (?)

I went with the load from Jeppe Nelsons—had a lovely (?) time. I stayed a[t] Nelsons for supper and Martha and I went down and watched Mr Babcock and Chas Fish move that barn. its 36 x 36 or 40 x 40 I dont know which but I do know its a pretty large one Babcock is the only man who had timbers long enough for it. We girls talked about barns and admired Mr Babcocks team which is the best team of its kind in Shelby Co—and possibly in Iowa—they took the prize at the fair last fall. They certainly are beauties. Then at supper time the men talked about school—that was great fun I assure you.

Have *tried* to phone you to find out how Mrs Bradley was but have failed every time

The picnic ribbon Bess made and then sent to her family in the spring of 1908.

Must close for now

Your little girl Bess

[Enclosure: A scarlet ribbon of taffeta measuring 1¾″ x 7½″. Where Bess has failed with her ink, she has stitched with white thread the identifying legend "Merrills Grove Dist No 7." The pin that held the badge to Bess's waist is intact.]

1. Bess learned from Olney and Fuller how to handle a rifle. When the crops were in and the weather turned cold, the trio was likely to spread out over a clean-

swept wheat field or trek through deep snow in the direction of Cuppy's Grove to shoot invading jackrabbits. Shooting was an art at which Bess developed such precision that when she migrated to South Dakota her skill took the brashness out of any young man who mistakenly assumed that an afternoon of target practice with her would automatically prove to be his prideful opportunity for showing off.

CMW: An interesting counterpoint to the above note written by Phil Gerber is this quotation from a letter written to Phil by Paul Corey on September 13, 1991: "Bess's stories of her prowess with a gun always puzzled me in her letters. I can remember her acquiring a 22, a small gun and I remember her taking a few practice shots under Olney's or Fuller's guidance, but that is all. Some of her sharpshooting stories I wondered about. Maybe she was just lucky or a natural marksman. But I felt that one time when she used a neighbor's gun, she was using a small gauge shotgun. And I also thought that she had 22 caliber shells loaded with shot. I remember having one or two of those and shooting some myself. But I've always had a hard time swallowing her shooting stories."

. . . .

JUNE 7, 1908 IRWIN, IOWA

To Mrs. M. M. Corey

Dear Ma,—Its about ten P.M. so perhaps you are writing a letter to me

Martha Nelson and I had agreed to wear our white dresses today if it was good weather but it rained last night and most of the forenoon. We got the work done up early then we had music (Charlie plays quite a bit since he found out why I got so lonesom for Myrtle) then played checkers till we were tired of that, Charlie helped me read a little in the Dane Bible, by that time the Mr & Mrs were asleep so the boys decided to have lunch and such a lunch as they served!! After lunch Gordon went out to play in the mud and after talking about postcards till we were tired of that I brought down "Now Or Never" and read a chapt. or two to get them interested then let C read it aloud. Hardly stopped for dinner or any thing else till half after three when Sorine and Millie came down. There is a little hard bottom creek down east of the school house so for a lark, (you needn't frown so) I put on old clothes and we girls went down for a wade—the girls removed their shoes and stockings at the house but I took a basin along and waited till I got to the bridge to pull off mine. The creek bed was hard and smooth, water swift and clear about one foot deep—there was an occasional hole or perhaps one filled with mud—we just had a fine time and just as it was getting exciting—Sorine had sat down, by accident of course, and just as I began to slip I let go my skirts and clawed the air to get my balance by which time my horrid skirts had absorbed considerable moisture—just then when all was excitement one exclamed "Glorymareau" one moaned "Oh, the dickens now what *shall* I do" or some thing like it and the third screamed "Crawdads! crawdads!" old sport bounded down the bank toward us and C and G hove in sight—it was too late to run so we had to stay and face the music—it wasn't so bad either for they showed us how to sail the basin brought for another purpose, rescued us from a large snapping turtle which they made angry and when he snapped threw mud in his mouth till his neck was three times its oringinal size. Of course we staid till late chore time then the girls didn't want to wait for me to dress my feet so we hiked up across the schoolyard and ran across the road to the shelter of the porch when horification! there stood the Ministers umbrella and rubbers—wonderments and suggestions were passed in horrified whispers—I looked in at the door—worse yet—the table was set for tea and the sittingroom door wide open—I heard some one coming and took tucks in my knees so my feet wouldnt show—it was Mr Scott and how his eyes twinkled. With coaxing and threats he was persuaded to go into the sitting room and close the door after him then I got a basin of water and rushed up stairs It took me about twenty minutes to wash and change from the skin out and when I got down they were all at table and instead of Rev Jensen it was Mr Peter Langland from California who is visiting friends and relatives in these parts He is an old maid gentleman—about thirty five years of age—owns a two hundred acre fruit farm in Cal. and is worth between fifteen and twenty thousand dollars they say—Well he staid till church time and I talked California for all there is in it—was most interested in the schools of which he knew nothing but volunteered to find out and send me information so I gave him my Marne address. My much interested friend Mr Scott advised me to take advantage of leapyear for they all think (?) Mr L much taken though I'm not conceited enough to think it serious but am eager for the coming of August so he will return home and send the promised information which he assured me would be no trouble at all.

There was quite a crowd at church in spite of the weather for it was

Rev Jensens last sermon before leaving for the old country next Friday It rained befor church was out but cleared off in time for us to go home.

There will be a surprise party on Rev Jensen Wednesday evening every one who goes is to give—put my name down for $1 the largest amount I saw in the book.

Thursday evening—Well will try and finish this if it takes all night.

Monday there was a little trouble in school but its all over now I guess. *Another* interested mamma had a word to say about the management of her little son.

Tuesday there was a Sunday School meeting out north that took several pupils out of school Tuesday evening we were all up to Soren Scotts, wait, no it was Monday evening.

Yesterday every pupil was in school and today all but one. Hope the weather stays good so they can keep it up.

Last evening the surprise came off The crowd from the south met here and from the north met at Justesens and when a certain word was passed over the phone all started.

Had intended to go flower hunting after school last evening to get wild roses for the party but Sorine was here and staid till supper time and she wouldn't go so I couldn't but found a armfull of very pretty ones right near the house after supper which I brought in and placed on the table to be ready when I was dressed. I wore my new white dress which is very becoming I think I wore the same jewelry I always do, my little gold ring and pin and gold watch then I thought those bright pink roses with asparagus to put in my hair and belt and on my dress would finish me off just right. I came down and made a boquet of three roses and some green—but that was all I got— just then the crowd came and the girls rushed upon me with cries of "Roses" "Roses" Of course I said "Help yourselves" and "*You know the rest.*"

Sorine didn't like it because I wore my new white and she didn't have hers ready to wear yet.

Well there were more than a hundred of us and the purse amounted to over twenty seven dollars, coffee and cake was served late in the evening and we played games till one oclock or perhaps a little after. Martha and I were the only two grown ups dressed all in white and we were together all evening. I would have had a *lovely* time if just two or three of my brothers were there as it was I played that Pete

Saul was my brother He is a cousin of the Nelson girls. I played all the time—Had Marthas three eldest brothers for partners quite a bit, but the partners I got most satisfaction out of being with were the lads who were my pupils last winter.

There was a great big piece of Denmark stepped on my dress I felt like canning him but he was hardly ripe enough.

Friday morning—your letter was rec'd yesterday—I think Miss Chapman a little dandy—am glad to hear that Grandma gets along so well—I used ink in writing to Fern—was careful not to say anything—she wrote to me you know and that wasn't so bad but she sent me a postal, a chicken picture and over it was written "Da these chickens say Dunham too" wasn't that a fright to send me through the mail? The mailman knows every teacher on this line & he's a regular old blatherskyte and any way who told Fern? you or the schoolma'am? A whole crowd saw that postal befor I did. I think you better be careful what your at.

I haven't written L or her mother either and I dont believe I will. If I attend S. S. and Institute it will make me eight months of school with out vacation and Mamma I'm getting so tired oh so tired. You know how I used to have a pain in my chest when it was damp or foggy? well this weather is hard on me Miss Chapman said it was catarrah of the lungs and said the only help was a dry warm climate— you needn't worry—its nothing serious—will try to overcome it and will be alright when it gets dry and warm. See why I talked California to Mr L?

Dont you think it would be better for me to come home a week from this evening as planned and go to Harlan the following Sunday for a week and take the June exams then come home for a month while you go have that operation then for me to go up the last week in July for two weeks, exams & Institute? Olney can help me this summer, it will be right in his line and what I pay him would help him out and I have only one monts wages to run me through the summer, The girls all plan a high old time in Summer S this year so if you decide for me to go I'll make the best of it. Mary L writes she isnt going & it seems to me best to stay home.

I would have liked to have been there to go boat riding.

Say don't you think it will be as well if Ethel dont go to Armstrongs so much

I've decided to cut out the dancing so its alright if I'm not home.

When you get Post Card by the bunch there are always some of the common lot and mine are down to those kind—wont send any more of them so there now. Have had a dose of letters of late—havent answered any of them.

Tell Chall I desperatly hungry for fish and I'll eat the biggest he can catch or give him a dollar but he musn't take time from his other work. Miss Anna Jensen who is to graduate from a school of music in Sac City next spring is home for vacation and as she is a fine musician I want Fuller to hear her well I must close so phone and let me know whether I'm going to S S or not,

Yours as ever

Bess

Corey Farm and Harlan SHELBY COUNTY, IOWA

School #4 in Marne, Clay Township, Shelby County, Iowa, close to the Corey farm, about 1909. Bess may have taught at this school; certainly the last names of the children are the same as her near neighbors. In the photograph (order not given) are: Jennie Haynes, Robert Haynes, Grace Haynes, Ethel Fish, Nels Nelson, Louise Sheef, Harry Sheef, Bert Christensen, Arnold Fredricksen, Freddie Fredrickson, Holger Sorensen, George Sorensen, Mattie Skow, and Eddie Damgaard.

School #9 in Marne, Clay Township, Shelby County, Iowa, across the road from the Corey farm, where Bess may have taught when she lived at home and most likely attended as a young girl. Paul Corey went to school here. He says, "I think I was in the sixth grade. The teacher was Gladys Wilson. Sitting on the edge of the porch is Teresa Sorenson. The standing girls, l-r, are Evelyn Murphy, Mildred Murphy, and Veronica Murphy. I'm the kid assuming the lotus position."

Bess (in the center) as she looked right after moving to South Dakota, October 1, 1910. (L-r) Emma Klemann, Fuller Corey (who had traveled to South Dakota to visit her), Bess, Oscar Walton, and Margaret Klemann.

As Bess had wished, she was permitted to come home and oversee the summer activities on Corey Farm while Margaret Corey went to Clarkson Memorial Hospital in Omaha, Nebraska, for surgery. Bess corresponded with her mother at that address during most of the summer, allowing us a rare glimpse into the daily routine on this working farm.

Because she recovered quickly from her surgery, Margaret was able to return to the farm and resume her duties in time for Bess to attend the annual summer institute for teachers in Harlan and write her examinations for teacher certification. It is in Harlan that she writes her last letter home for another year, because she appears to have lived at home while she taught during the 1908–1909 year close to Corey Farm once again (probably at #9, where both her brother Olney and her sister Ethel would later teach), but it could also have been Marne School #4, judging by the familiar names of the children in the photograph on page 161. This is unfortunate, because it was during this time period that she was making definite plans to strike out on her own as soon as she reached legal age of twenty-one. The stories of those who had left Iowa to homestead in South Dakota appealed to her, so in June 1909, she set out by train from Harlan. Her schoolteacher friend Lida Smith accompanied her; and her friend George Stewart (on whom she'd long had an unrequited crush) came to the depot to see them off.

JULY 8, 1908 MARNE, IOWA

To Mrs. M. M. Corey

Dear Mamma,—Will start this this evening and try to get it finished before mail time tomorrow morning. I am so rushed most of the time between five A.M. and ten P.M. that I only hit the high places so you'll have to 'scuse all mistakes.

Chall reached home safely the other day and I've worn my glasses quite a bit mostly when there aren't many around

That evening after you went I heard Paul howling bloody murder and went out to the gate to see what was the trouble—Paul was coming up the plank rubbing his south east ear and crying more because he was angry than hurt. I asked him what was the matter and he said "I fell down and of course Ethel had to come and fall on top of me."

Yesterday was his birthday. He received a pretty postal from Grandma and Ethel made him a hemstitched handkerchief with his initial in one corner. He came in about ten oclock in the morning a sight to behold his clothes were just plastered with mud. He had been sitting on the to[p] board of the hog pen fence and his feet slipped and he fell off into a mud hole. we were going to change his clothes but found we had to scrape a good layer of mud of him to above his waist and then give him a bath for the mud was so thin that when he lit feet down ward the mud went right up inside his clothes. He was sitting on an over turned pail in the back kitchen waiting for me to finish him off and after sitting in silence with a most woeful countenance for a few minutes he said "I just knew I'd have some such luck as this on my birthday"

After dinner I heard him yell and saw Fuller run to the barn. They say Paul was fooling about Nells coalt and the coalt kicked him twice and knocked the wind out of him. Rob asked if he didn't know the coalt would kick and he said "Yes I knew she'd kick me but I didn't spose em little feet could hurt anyone" He came to the house about ten minutes later and I asked him what he was making such a noise about and he looked up at me a instant then said "Bess, can't I blow soap bubbles?" That was all I ever got out of him about it.

We washed and scrubbed yesterday, baked bread, churned and

picked currents today. Mrs Lawliss was here yesterday and today in the afternoon picking currents on shares. I've sold Mrs Lanigan a twelve quart pail for fifty cents

The boys have finished rigging the hay barn and it works fine they put up five loads this after noon. We rustle out at five in the morning and they are going to plow corn till ten each morning then put up hay for the rest of the day.

Fuller took off nine pigs yesterday were very light brought $56.50 and weighed 1135 lb I think it was at any rate he only got five cents.

The little cow that aint the Fool but lost her first calf has another it fell in the creek but the boys pulled it out and it seems all right they say.

You need not worry about those potatoes in the garden they are doing as well as they ever did we got twelve potatoes out of one hill that would *almost average* as large as your fist.

Olney reached home safely about nine thirty this evening. He had been at Copleys all afternoon I guess. Copleys leave for the west in a few days, will sell their good[s] at auction on Saturday rec'd a card from Irma saying that her mother had between twenty five and thirty yards of rag capet as good as new that you could have at fifteen cents per, if you wanted it. I wrote her that you were away and I would not be able to get word to you and back again so would have to let it go.

Fuller rec'd a pretty postal from Rose today and I one from Mary L. Well good night its half after eleven.

Friday Morning—Mrs Lawless is picking currents this morning will just have her leave one or two good bushes for sause. I'm going after the black and white currents when I finish this. If I can get all the currents finished this week I'll be satisfied even if I don't get all the ironing done.

Ethel and the boys all work fine—the fiddle and horn have hardly been touched since you went away We havent the crackers and cookies yet but think they will get here by the time you get home

In Haste From

Your Little Girl Bess.

Fuller has a sore hand but think it is getting along alright—have been doing it up in soap and sugar.

JULY 10, 1908 MARNE, IOWA

To Mrs. M. M. Corey, Clarkson Memorial Hospital, 1716 Dodge St., Omaha, Neb.

Dear Mamma,—Hope this will find you improving rapidly. Don't worry about anything just rest and get well God can take care of us better than you could if you were here and I've trusted him to take care of you and I think He is doing a pretty good job of it all around.

The red currents are all picked now but one bush left for sauce— have twenty four quarts in can and a small batch ready to put on in the morning. I picked the white and black currents this afternoon had a fourteen quart pail most full of white ones and about two and one half or three quarts of black—that finishes the currents for now though the black ones will have to be gone over again later. I am just canning every thing up straight for there has been so much to do I've been afraid if I stoped to bother with jell or jam that some of the rest of the fruit would spoil while I was at it and I don't know exactly which jars to put it in any way.

It is almost half after ten and the boys are just getting in. —Well it's later, I stopped to put some other sheets on Toads bed—they're all in bed now. It looks rainy to night and they were bound to put the last load of hay from the north fourty into the barn before stopping they didn't get home with their last load till half after eight and did their chores before putting it in. They were awful tired but *so* jolly— you just auto hear them sing, laugh and crack jokes right up till they were all in bed and now how still—just heavy breathing in every room.

Rob does fine but to night he was so tired that when Olney got to teasing him he gave a back hand lick that most knocked Olney out of his chair and then began to cry but Olney said like Paul did about the Little Roxie "I knew he'd hit me but I didn't spose 'em little hands would hurt any one" then Rob laughed with the rest of us.

I dont like to have the boys out so late especially Chall for they are all up about five every morning but I guess its just for tonight.

My!!! We'll be glad when you get back—the machinery *will* jump cogs *once* in a while with out you to oil and watch it.

Twigs[1] got to sleeping pretty loud this noon and Paulie excused himself from the table to go out and ask him if it was stomach ache or what was troubling him which amused Mrs Lawless who was here to dinner.

I've been going to bed at ten and getting up at five—I guess it was much later than ten last eve and is eleven now. am getting toughened up so I don't mind the long hard days so much as I thought I should but was a little sleepy this after noon.

Will stop now and tell you in the morning whether it rains or not.

[July 11] No it didn't rain last night and we are all hard at it this morning.

Rob went up to Armstrongs this morning early to see about, borrowing their side delivery rake. He ask Ed if they would be useing it soon and Ed said "No you can have it any time" and never waited to be asked for it. It will save them lots of driving and they think they can put up eight loads this after noon. Olney is plowing sod—think he will finish and start to plow that piece that is so small the third time today—They'll plow that one piece four times I guess

Chall is chore boy does pretty well for so small a boy—is rather steady by jerks.

Finished canning the red currents had about twenty eight quarts. The last can wasnt quite full. Will finish the others today.

Must close

Yours Truly

Bess

1. The family dog (PG). According to Paul Corey, "a black part terrier, part pit-bull with brown markings."

．．．

JULY 13, 1908 MARNE, IOWA

To Mrs. M. M. Corey

Dear Mamma,—The currents are all in can—there are about twenty eight quarts of red, six of white and two of black.

Fuller, Rob and Chall went to S. S. at Rorbeck yester morning and the rest of us went to church at Monroe in the afternoon. It made me scratch to get the right duds for each one of 'em—I havent the hang of things yet exactly. Rev Wright asked for your address so he could write you—Olney says he hopes Rev Wright wont write you for money thinking when you are sick you'll give more.

There was quite a large crowd out yesterday and I was quite bothered after church to find myself the center of *every*thing—some asked why you weren't there it seemed queere to see the rest without you, some asked if you were sick and so on. Mrs Curtis[1] said to send you her love and best wishes said she hoped and prayed you would return to us well and strong.

Armstrongs and others were there—possibly to discover the identity of the party I talked to over the phone but as he wasn't there they got left that time. Paulie says "Bess: phone George that he brought the crowd if he wasnt there himself." I thought that just about hit it.

The boys promise not to work so late after this—wouldnt have before only it looked so stormy it hasnt stormed yet though.

We girls have bread to bake and some ironing and mending to do to-day—have already mended my "black cheese cloth with white pimples on it" and fixed that white skirt for Ethel.

Saturday I was just about sick you know but worked at the currents and in the afternoon we scrubbed the kitchen, back-kitchen and four porches.

Say how long do you expect to be up there? I wish you could write and tell me what about Fullers overalls—I've got it mixed and what about Paul's, the two pair he has been wearing seem pretty badly gone where all overalls go.

We girls will start to Rorbeck in a few minutes. So long and good luck to you

Your Little Girl Bess

Rec'd four pretty postals last week—yours for one.

[On the envelope is a handwritten list:]

No 3

overalls

Dr Simmons

Hog check

B. B.

My advance check

(?)

Roxie

cookies

[Enclosed with the letter was a standard receipt from A. C. Knudsen & Co., General Merchandise, Rorbeck, Iowa, stating "30 cents for rivets." On the back of the folded receipt is Bess's expense list:]

check book	.25
Buggy brid[l]es	2.60
Breast collars	5.40
Violin tunes	.18
Gloves	.95

1. A Mrs. Curtis is identified on page 409 of *Bachelor Bess* as the choir leader at the Monroe Township Methodist Church, where the Corey family usually attended services (CMW).

. . . .

JULY 15, 1908 MARNE, IOWA

To Mrs. M. M. Corey

Dear Ma,—I just opened the desk and there on top of every thing lay the enclosed card which I had forgotten to look for.

Yesterday Fuller mowed some more hay down and he and Rob plowed corn—Olney worked in the garden and yard—helped get the ducks broke to stay in the other yard.

This morning early Olney started on his next job which is to help George Neff and Fred Fell put up eighty acres of hay.

It was never decided who should go to the show till this morning. All three boys wanted to go—Fuller said Ethel should go if any one went and Rob wouldn't leave me here alone with just Paul so Rob and Chall staid at home to plow and Fuller and Ethel went. Is not that a feather in Roberts cap?

Ethel had at least a dozen grease spots on her blue skirt some as large as your hand so I had to wash, dry, and iron it this morning so they didn't get started till more than a quarter after eight. Fuller promised to take the best kind of care of Ethel so she is all right. She wore my cravanet in case of rain for it is threatening some.

I have socks and overalls to mend today have three little boils along side my nose—can hardly wear my glasses and my eyes are dancing jigs

The freight came Monday P.M. Armstrongs brought it out. 80 c.

Uncle Chris has catarahal apendecitis bad thought at first an operation necessary but not now.

Martha Nelson and Mrs Wheeler rang up yesterday

Yours In Haste

Bess

. . . .

JULY 16, 1908 MARNE, IOWA

To Mrs. M. M. Corey

Dear Ma,—Your postals rec'd each day. I dont like the sound of "better in some ways."

Have used up the last of my letter paper so have borrowed(?) some of your note paper.

It rained here yesterday afternoon quite a shower but not in Marne or Atlantic so they say. Fuller and Ethel got home between eleven and twelve last evening—it struck twelve befor I got to sleep. It rained quite hard between the time they got home and morning.

The boys worked late yesterday noon and finished the corn across the creek have only twenty acres at the north fourty to finish now—will only take them a day and a half. and as it rained befor we finished dinner yesterday the boys F. R. and P. all went to sleep and slept all afternoon I scrubbed my hair and mended. You should just see my hair this morning so light and fuzzy—is trying its best to curl all over

Mrs Sorensen called up last evening—Mr Sorensen is much better.

Got weighed yesterday—have lost ten pounds more—weigh 184 lbs now—am feeling fine.

I don't believe I told you yesterday that in the morning when Bill Jacobs went past he called and ask Rob if he was going to the show and Rob said "Nope—takes too much money to go every time." I thought I saw Bill *smile*.

Jennie Noon passed as Ethel and I were digging potatoes one morning and stopped to talk a while. Those potatoes are fine—more than a bushel in some rows

Must get Robert some overalls as he has only a pair and a half now.

Well I must close—can't send you a cookie this morning—they're too soft so send lots of love. Must churn.

Oh yes Paul rec'd a postal from Rose yestermorning and I a letter from Grandma Aunt Mary is not improving—has given up all work and is under the doctors care.

From

Your Little Girl Bess

. . . .

JULY 16, 1908 MARNE, IOWA

To Mrs. M. M. Corey

Dear Ma,—Your letter rec'd this morning. Will procede to answer all questions ask through mail heretofore.

The order pinned in Challs pocked rec'd. Letter to Rose sent. Soap kettle taken care of. Some one threw a hammer to Fuller it hit the palm of his hand near the root of his little finger causing a bruise which gathered and tried to swell up and look like something. We did it up in soap and sugar for a day or two after opening it.—is alright now. My hand was dog bit is alright now but will leave a scar. Have sent you the card you lost in the writing desk. I got those cards off alright—though a trifle late. Olney hasn't sent a card to Uncle S not that I know of any way—and is away from home now and I dont know the address. No the colts name is Maud or mud or something. M W & Co's freight rec'd Monday evening. Twenty eight loads of hay up and three acres (I think) to put up yet—guess its more than three acres— Rob said about ten loads *perhaps*. Harvesting a ways off yet & one or two days corn plowing to do yet. Some of the garden is in the ducks but it must be alright—they seem to flurish and what we've had to eat was alright. so I guess its all alright—sweet corn higher than the fence. There now, I guess all your questions are answered—No—Hog check sent in. There now they're all answered. You needn't scold a fellow when he's doing the best he can—I'm *so* tired at night and my eyes blur so and in the morning I'm in a rush and know something is let slide while I'm writing and you needn't think you can scold or blame me even in your mind and that far off very much with out my knowing it. I was with you those nights when you were sorting old clothes—I would go to bed tired oh so tired and would wake up once in a while almost crying—with a sence of being blamed for what I was not to blame for and in the morning would wake up tired and won-der what I had done to be scolded for and would feel uncomfortable about it for some time. I didn't think it was sorting old clothes all the time though. You said I was more stupid than Ethel could be if she tried I believe or something of the sort.

I just wish I could correspond with some Dr or nurse or other up there—the little happenings there would interest me and I'm sure I could make some of the happenings here interesting to them if they could slide over the mistakes when I'm in a hurry.

Have heard from my exam—only got a third—too low in Grammar and physiology. Will write in July exam and Ethel and Paul will go to Atlantic for a few days or a week.

Paul the little snipe not only talks Dane but is teaching it to Twigs. He asked me the other day for some cookies and then thanked me in Danish. I replied in Danish "No no you must talk English." He went on out to play with Twigs and when Twigs barked at him I heard him say in Danish just like and old Dane "No, no, Twigs, you must talk English" It sounded so funny. Poor little Twigs made a jump in the hay today of about five feet and broke one of his fore legs. He had jumped much farther and never been hurt and he lit in the hay this time too but suppose he must have landed differantly the last time he cries with it so pitifuly by spells.

There it strikes eleven and I must bake bread and wash tomorrow—have been having another little spell of indigestion hope I'll be better in the morning but I must go to roost.

Good Night

From Bess.

. . . .

JULY 20, 1908 MARNE, IOWA

To Mrs. M. M. Corey

Dear Ma,—Robert rec'd your card and one from Grandma at the same time I rec'd one from Lida Smith—a regular jimsizzor—picture of a large rather good looking woman with Merry Widow Hat—a rather small gent on step latter reaching up—verse underneath says

Ah, sweetheart don't you know

What I am driving at?

Why, my love for *you* is as big

As—your Merry Widow Hat.

If she had written "Little Dane" underneath it wouldn't have been planer. Lida is at Sarahs—having a fine time—wanted me to write at once—I did—told her all the latest and that I would show the "Little Dane" the post card and give him her address.

The boys finished the hay late Saturday evening—thirty eight loads—the last load was large as two ordinary ones.

Paulie has been haying also—can not you see him? Hickory shirt, blue patched overalls and straw hat, hay poles and other haying machinery—stacking grass in the back yard—can't you see him shove back his hat and scratch his little white head as he eyes criticly a well finished stack or views a broken bit of machinery and exclaims, "Well Gee'ruslem"

We were all at the Rorbeck S S picnic yesterday—Fuller Rob—Ethel and Chall went to Sunday School. Fuller came home to dinner, the others staid—Fuller and Theadore rode wheels up after dinner and Olney, Paul and I went up in the buggy and brought Ethel and Chall home with us. Coming home Chall sat on Olneys lap, Paul on Ethels and I sat on the third seat and drove. There was an immense crowd—a whole school of Fish—was unable to determine whether bullheads or suckers—didn't try to catch any. Were all invited up to Armstrongs for ice cream and cake last evening—Fuller Rob and Chall went but I had a headache so the rest of us staid at home

Did I tell you I received a letter from "Little Petra" and that Marie Jensen called up the other evening?

Olney has gone back at his haying—is among a jolly crowd that don't love to hurt themselves by over work

Yours Bess

[Written sideways by the date on page 1, before the salutation:] Fuller is going to Walnut—will have him mail your shoes. We are all well but busy. My accounts are all straight and up to date. E. F. C.

. . . .

JULY 21, 1908 MARNE, IOWA

To Mrs. M. M. Corey

Dear Mamma,—Yours of Sun. rec'd yesterday. We are all well. Fuller went to Walnut yesterday forenoon, and as they didn't plow corn in the afternoon it will not be finished till this noon.

I phoned Mrs Sorensen and she said when you got to Marne to phone them from the depot and if none of us were there to get you that she or Mr Sorensen would drive down after you as you would have moving enough without walking up there. She also thinks you had better stay a night or two in town before coming home.

Our first picking of black berries yesterday—about three pints I think—had them for dinner.

had a nice letter from Ida W yesterday and a letter from Grand Fodder with clearance and transfer cards.

We are going to wash and scrub today and iron and bake bread tomorrow. Get blue? Well I guess not! Every thing goes as slick as a greased pig. Oh I suppose some little bits of missmanagament will rear up to the surface after you get home but as I started in as a green hand nothing else could be expected

Am very anxious for you to get home for if your eyes are good and you could spare the time from the mending and such you could read to me and help me get ready for the exam.

Please write us when to meet you. Fuller says for you to come on an evening train if you intend to come right out home as it will be so much pleasanter.

Will not write again if you plan to come on Thurs.

With Love

Bess.

Paulie starts up occasionly with "I believe I hear mamma coming" or "I hear mamma coming home"

. . . .

AUGUST 11, 1908 HARLAN, IOWA

To Mrs. E. O. Corey

Dear Ma, Will take time for a note. I don't know where to begin as the train goes out soon and I'd like to "Have it over with" you know.

I reached Harlan about two thirty, on Saturday, I believe and went straight to Smiths they were not at home so I left my suit case and package on the porch and went over to Murpheys where I secured board—went up town and enrolled—Oh wait a minute till I finish this apple—Well its finished.—and got our [Chautauqua] tickets—then went out to Smiths after my suit case then rested here till supper time. After supper we went to Chautauqua.

There are quite a few of us here now. Mr Shabin, Mr Bonney, Mary and I beside Frank Murphey and we have some fun. Am awful short of money—board higher than I expected—rainy weather caused me to purchase a parasol—had forgotten I owed a bill at Nielsens. so please send me some or I will have to jump aboard bill. It is raining and we didn't go to Chautauqua but Joe and Mary are cutting up so I most cant think straight.

Hope you are well

Your little girl

Bess

Bibliography

The abbreviation SHSI indicates a source that was once in the possession of Phil Gerber but is now located in Special Collections at the State Historical Society of Iowa, Iowa City.

Arndt, Roma Lehnhardt. *Walnut Memoirs: A History of Walnut, Iowa*. Iowa Falls: General Publishing and Binding, 1987.

Atlas of Shelby County, Iowa, Containing Maps of the Townships of the County. N.p., 1911.

[Centennial Recognition Committee]. *A History of the Shelby, Iowa Community from Early Times until Its Centennial Year of 1970.* N.p., 1970.

Compendium of History and Biography of Cass County, Iowa. Chicago: Henry Taylor, 1906.

Corey, Paul. Letters to Philip L. Gerber, various dates. SHSI.

———. "My Four Brothers and Two Sisters." Typescript, n.p. n.d., SHSI.

Field, Homer H., and Joseph R. Reed. *History of Pottawattamie County, Iowa, from the Earliest Historic Times to 1907.* Chicago: S. J. Clarke, 1907.

Gerber, Philip L. "Bachelor Bess: How She Began." 16-page typescript with photocopies of family photos and letters, apparently submitted to *Palimpsest* in 1991. SHSI.

———, ed. *Bachelor Bess: The Homesteading Letters of Elizabeth Corey, 1909–1919.* Iowa City: University of Iowa Press, 1990.

———. "'I Could Write a Book': Paul and Elizabeth Corey." *Books at Iowa* 52 (April 1990): 12–52.

———. "Those First Chautauquas: Bess Corey in Harlan, 1905–06." Unpublished 16-page typescript. SHSI.

———. "Written on the Run: The Unconventional Autobiography of Elizabeth Corey." Unpublished 14-page typescript of speech apparently presented at MLA conference in 1991. SHSI.

———, and Paul Corey. "Queries for Paul Corey: Iowa and Corey-Family References." Typescript, [1988], SHSI.

Harlan High School Annuals, 1894, 1895, 1896, 1989. SHSI.

"Harlan Newspapers Souvenir—'Centennial Special.'" Special section of the *Harlan News Advertiser*, July 2, 1979. SHSI.

History of Cass County, Iowa. Springfield, Illinois: Continental Historical Company, 1884.

The Industrial American, Being a Story of Harlan, Her Past Growth and Future Prosperity. [Harlan, Iowa]: A. T. Cox, 1892.

Iowa State Census. 1905. Accessed through ancestry.com.

Nelson, Margaret. Letters to Philip L. Gerber, various dates. SHSI.

Pike, Edna M. "Information for Phillip Gerber." Handwritten note, map, and family history charts, [1991?]. SHSI.

Shelby County, Iowa. District 3, Clay Township. School records, 1905–1908. SHSI.

———. School Library Records, Douglas Township, 1901–1913. SHSI.

Shelby County Republican. Originals at Harlan Historical Museum, Harlan, Iowa.

Shelby Township Schools. Minutes Book, 1903–1917. Shelby County Historical Museum, Harlan, Iowa.

Shupe, Verlee. Letter to Philip Gerber. November 18, 1991. SHSI.

Standard Atlas of Shelby County, Iowa. Chicago: Geo. A. Ogle, 1899.

Swanson, Ruth R. (Nelson). Letter to Philip L. Gerber, undated [1994?]. SHSI.

U.S. Federal Census. 1900 and 1910. Accessed through ancestry.com.

White, Edward S. *Past and Present of Shelby County, Iowa.* Indianapolis: B. F. Bowen, 1915.

Index

Note: Where a person's last name is not included or is not clear from the context, the index entry includes only a first name. Where a last name is in brackets, I am fairly sure of the identification. Where the identification is merely probable, I have put a *see* or *see also* reference (CMW).

Bohlander family, 58
Bohlander, Mrs. *See* Rosa Wunder
Boland, James, 119
Bonny, Mr., 174
Bradly/Bradley, Mrs., 149, 154
Bremer family, 27
Brown, Clarence, 13
Brown family, 84, 88, 98
Brown, Florence, 146
Brown, Johnny, 153
Brown, Lewis, 84, 89
Brown, Lona, 72
Brown, May, 84, 89
Brown, Miss, 42
Brown, Mr., 85, 86, 90, 101, 104, 109
Brown, Mrs., 98
Brown, Nourmal, 146
Brown, Professor, 14
Brown, Seward, 98
Brown, Will, 84
Bruce, Mr., 15
Buckley family, 102
Buckley, Frank, 83, 102
[Buckley?], Martha, 102
[Buckley?], Mildred, 102
Buckley, Mrs. Sam. *See* Martha Wever
Buckley, Samuel, 102, 103, 104n
Bunton, Georgie, 10
Burke, Edmond, 20
Byam, C. J., 44
Byers, Beatrice, 95

C——, 137, 139, 146, 147, 14
C——, Mr., 16, 18
C——, Mrs., 17
Carey, Glen, 10, 20
Carey, Theo, 10
Cass County (Iowa): ethnic diversity, 1, 2, 6
Center School, 66
Chambles, Lauretta. *See* Lauretta Chamblis

Chamblis family, 20
Chamblis, Lauretta, 11, 13
Chapman, Miss, 159
Charlie, 133, 138, 141, 142, 146, 148, 151, 154, 156
chautauquas, 30, 32, 32n, 121, 126, 152, 174
Chicago (Illinois), 26, 75
children, 135; accidents, 28, 29, 82; anecdotes about, 75–76, 141–142, 152–153, 164, 166–167, 172, 173; births of, 18, 138; deaths of, 28, 29 chores, 7, 12, 18, 28. *See also* Elizabeth Corey—farm and domestic chores
Chris, 133
Christensen, Bert, 161
Christensen, C. H., 139
Christensen, Chris, 142
Christensen family, 27, 132
Christensen, Sam, 149
Christensen, Sorn, 59
Christensen, Walter, 132, 133
Christian Science. *See* religion— Christian Science
church. *See* religion
Cissna, Minnie, 20
Clarinda (Iowa) Asylum, 135
Clarkson Memorial Hospital, 163, 166
Cobb, Dr., 99
Colman, 18
Cook, Harlan, 57
Cook, Henry, 57
Copley, Bert, 18, 20
Copley, Charlie, 18
[Copley?], Ella, 13
Copley family, x, xii, xiii, 13, 57n, 59, 165
Copley, George, 91
Copley, Helen, 9, 13, 14
Copley, Ida, 13, 16
Copley, Irma, 9, 12, 13, 14, 42, 58, 165

Copley, Mary, 9, 13, 14. *See also* Mary
    Copley Hummer
Copley, Mr., 18, 20, 22, 54. *See also*
    Mr. C___
Copley, Mrs., 9, 14, 19, 23, 59, 72, 86
Copley, Reba, 16
Copley, William (Jr.), 9
Copley, William (Sr.), 9
Corey, Anna Mariah (grandma), xxi,
    6, 30, 40, 72, 86, 108, 119, 164, 171,
    172
Corey, Challenge Richard "Chall"
    (brother), 7, 8n, 78, 84, 135, 151,
    160, 164, 167, 169, 171
Corey, Edwin O. (father), xi, 1, 4–5, 6,
    14, 24, 26, 30n, 33n, 34n, 84, 127n
Corey, Elizabeth: adventurousness,
    63, 100; appearance and weight,
    19, 41, 48, 50, 64, 75, 79, 82, 94,
    95, 99, 101, 107, 142, 145, 153, 170;
    boarding, x, xiii–xiv, 9, 26–27,
    44–45, 84, 125, 129, 135, 148,
    149, 150; boarding room descrip-
    tions, 28, 47, 86, 112, 114; busi-
    ness of teacher's day, 88, 94–95,
    101, 105, 106, 107, 118, 121, 132,
    133, 149, 150, 154, 156–158; can-
    ning and cooking, 55, 68, 166;
    and chautauquas, 30, 32, 34; and
    Christian Science, 31–32, 33, 33n;
    church attendance and thoughts
    about religion, 13, 14, 31–33, 53,
    55, 57, 58, 59, 62–75, 77, 87, 95,
    99, 107, 121, 124–125, 131–132,
    133, 136, 139, 140, 148, 149, 152,
    153, 157–158, 167–168, 173; cloth-
    ing, 12, 17, 18, 23, 28, 32, 37, 39,
    41, 43, 50, 51, 53, 54–55, 62, 64,
    66, 83, 88, 89, 93, 95, 97, 99–100,
    107, 115, 118, 122, 144, 146, 156,
    157, 158; at Corey Farm, 1–8, 111,
    128, 161–174; desire to farm rather

than teach, xvii, 43, 90, 167; eating habits, food, and meals, 12, 31,
42, 46, 51, 52–53, 60, 66, 71–72, 74,
86, 91, 108, 109, 113–116, 118, 119,
120, 122, 124, 131, 133, 134, 139,
153–154, 160, 173; education of, ix,
xii, 9–24, 25–43; exam taking and
exam giving, xii–xiii, 18–24, 37, 40,
41, 42, 43, 104, 116, 123, 159, 172;
expenses and spending habits, 11,
12, 15, 17, 18, 22, 23, 24, 28, 29, 30,
32, 36, 37, 38, 39, 42, 43, 51, 53, 54,
58, 60, 61, 63, 64, 72, 83, 84, 103,
105, 110, 118, 122, 133, 135, 141, 144,
149, 151–153, 169, 174–175; farm
and domestic chores, 7, 12, 18, 23,
28, 48, 50, 57, 81, 83, 144, 148, 149,
164–174; father's death, xi, 26, 107;
and games, 66–67, 70, 132, 139,
140, 158–159; in Harlan, 25–43,
62–63, 111–127, 144, 174–175; healing of others, 31, 33; health and
hygiene, 18, 31, 61–63, 75, 77, 94,
97, 99, 103, 107, 114, 115, 120, 124,
125, 127, 131–132, 133, 142, 146–
147, 150, 153, 159, 169, 171; helping
others, 68–69, 78, 80, 90, 148; and
holidays, 30–32, 52–53, 57, 59, 61,
93, 94–95, 136, 143, 152; home-
sickness, 35, 40, 43, 50, 51, 53, 59,
61, 69, 91, 116, 119, 121, 123, 149,
152; homesteading, ix, xvii, xxi,
100, 162; honesty, 19, 49–50, 61,
62, 90; in Irwin, 128–160; interactions with parents of her students,
xvii, 47–50, 58, 61–62, 68–69,
79–80, 87, 88, 91–93, 96–97, 121–
122, 158; interactions with poten-
tial beaus, 31, 35, 36, 37, 38, 40, 52,
57, 60, 67, 71–72, 73–75, 79, 82,
90–91, 95, 98, 106, 108–109, 117,
122–123, 125, 126, 132, 133, 136,

Other Bur Oak Books of Interest

A Bountiful Harvest
The Midwestern Farm Photographs
   of Pete Wettach, 1925–1965
   By Leslie A. Loveless

Buxton
A Black Utopia in the Heartland
   by Dorothy Schwieder, Joseph
   Hraba, and Elmer Schwieder

Central Standard
A Time, a Place, a Family
   By Patrick Irelan

Harker's Barns
Visions of an American Icon
   Photographs by Michael P. Harker
   Text by Jim Heynen

Harker's One-Room Schoolhouses
Visions of an Iowa Icon
   Photographs by Michael P. Harker
   With an essay by Paul Theobald

An Iowa Album
A Photographic History, 1860–1920
   By Mary Bennett

Iowa Stereographs
Three-Dimensional Visions of the Past
   By Mary Bennett and Paul C. Juhl

Letters of a German American Farmer
Jürnjakob Swehn Travels to America
   By Johannes Gillhoff

Neighboring on the Air
Cooking with the KMA Radio
   Homemakers
   By Evelyn Birkby

Nothing to Do but Stay
My Pioneer Mother
   By Carrie Young

Picturing Utopia
Bertha Shambaugh and the Amana
   Photographers
   By Abigail Foerstner

Sunday Afternoon on the Porch
Reflections of a Small Town in Iowa,
   1939–1942
   Photographs by Everett W. Kuntz
   Text by Jim Heynen